NICODEMOS
YOU MUST
BE BORN AGAIN

**Pastor Midagbodji Ablam
(Abraham)**

Kingdom Publishers

Nicodemos You Must Be Born Again
Copyright© Pastor Midagbodji Ablam (Abraham)

All rights reserved. No part of this book may be
reproduced in any form by photocopying or any
electronic or mechanical means, including information
storage or retrieval systems, without permission in
writing from both the copyright owner and the publisher
of the book. The right of Pastor Midagbodji Ablam (Abraham) to be
identified as the author of this work has been asserted by him in
accordance with the Copyright, Designs and Patents Act
1988 and any subsequent amendments thereto.
A catalogue record for this book is available from the
British Library.

All Scripture Quotations have been taken from the New International Version and
the King James Version of the Bible.

ISBN: 978-1-913247-69-0

1st Edition by Kingdom Publishers
Kingdom Publishers
London, UK.

You can purchase copies of this book from any leading bookstore or
email **contact@kingdompublishers.co.uk**

DEDICATION

This book is dedicated to our Lord and Saviour, Jesus Christ whose inspiration has made the vision of this book a reality. Again, I dedicate this book to the Apostles of Jesus Christ and the early apostolic fathers who laboured in defending the *truth* in spite of the danger of persecution. Finally, it is dedicated to the true ministers of the Gospel who are still keeping the Faith that was once delivered to the Apostles.

ACKNOWLEDGEMENTS

I thank my Lord and Saviour, Jesus Christ, who through mercy and compassion took me from a sinful pit, to start a new thing with me that could be seen, touched and read.

I thank my wife, Assilamehou Akossiwoa, and my daughters, Midagbodji Ayawa Gentile and Freda Adu Yeboah, who worked together with me throughout.

I thank the members of *Holy Faith Pentecostal Church* in the land of Udine, Italy, and the members of the *Holy Faith Pentecostal Church* in Kegue Zogbedzi, Lome, Togo, whose effort and prayers have made this vision a reality.

Finally, my appreciation goes to prayer Pillars and prayer Warriors who stand in the gap by praying and interceding for the body of Christ worldwide.

Unless otherwise indicated, Scripture is taken from the King James \version of the Bible.

CONTENTS

INTRODUCTION

There was a man of the Pharisees, named Nicodemus, a ruler of the Jews. The same came to Jesus by night, and said unto him, Rabbi, we know that thou art a teacher come from God. For no man can do these miracles, that thou doest, except God be with him. Jesus answered and said unto him, verily, verily, I say unto thee, except a man be born again, he cannot see the kingdom of God. Nicodemus saith unto him, how can a man be born when he is old? Can he enter the second time into his mother's womb, and be born? Jesus answered, verily, verily, I say unto thee, except a man be born of water and of the Spirit, he cannot enter into the kingdom of God. That which is born of the flesh is flesh, and that which is born of the Spirit is spirit. (John 3:1-6)

The real message of the Lord's sufferings on the cross is missing from the Kingdom's message and is making the Lord's suffering of no effect. The purpose of the cross was the establishment of God's kingdom here on earth and, just as every kingdom has an entrance, the focus of Jesus Christ was to bring man out from this evil world into the kingdom of God, which He came to establish on earth. He said *in me, you will find peace but in the world, you will have tribulations, because I am the Way, the Truth and the Life....* (John 14:6)

The title of this book, <u>*Nicodemus, you must be Born Again,*</u> is a complete self-interpreted message to the children and the men of God, who have been in ministry for many years and claim to be doing well in ministry but still need to be born again. Some have promoted themselves to be Bishops, Apostles, Pastors, Prophets and Evangelists but are still looking for that which would make them great in the sight of men. In the eyes of God, they are like Nicodemus, needing to be born again of water and of the Spirit in Jesus' name for the remission of their sins.

Since Jesus Christ is not the author of confusion, He has set certain people apart in the Bible, to give us an understanding of who could be a Nicodemus. Such people are those that need to be born again in order to join the people of God who are on the right direction to heaven according to the example He gives in Matthew chapter seven.

Now, since there is a gateway or a door that leads into every kingdom or house, the Lord's main concern was to give the key that opens His kingdom to His chosen servants. He chose Apostle Peter among them and gave him the *keys to the Kingdom*. Before Jesus Christ told Peter that He would give him the *Keys* to the Kingdom, He had already spoken to Nicodemus that, unless a man is born of water and of the Spirit, he could not see or enter into the kingdom of God. So *the key* that opens the Kingdom's gate, is the *Word* of God to man that he must be born again of water (baptised) and of the Holy Spirit; if not, he cannot see or enter into the kingdom of God.

As was the position with Nicodemus, that he could not let him enter into the kingdom of God, so it is today. Titles and positions in the Church today are all useless without the real message of being *born again* of water and of the Spirit in Jesus' name. Many church leaders are focusing on miracles, signs and wonders, and some even fast for long periods to receive the Kingdom's power. Such do receive this by faith because God honours His Word. Today, many believers are healed during crusades due to their faith but are still not saved according to the *key* of entering into the Kingdom.

The Lord told the seventy disciples who returned to Him with testimonies of how demons were subject to them through His name, that they should not be happy at the signs and wonders they performed in His name, but should be happy because their names have been written in heaven. It is one thing when prayers are answered in the name of Jesus Christ, and another thing to have salvation through the name of Jesus.

Jesus said, *"That day many shall say unto me in your name we cast out demons, healed the sick and did many wonderful things but I'll say unto them depart from me, for I know you not, you who did not righteousness"*. (Matthew 7:24)

We can do all things in the name of Jesus Christ, which may promote the Kingdom but we will lose our salvation if we do not enter through the right door. Job 25:4-6 poses the question: *How... can man be justified with God? or how can he be clean that is born of a woman? Behold even to the moon, and it shineth not, yea, the stars are not pure in his sight. How much less man, that is a worm? And the son of man, which is a worm?*

Every man must answer this question. Jesus, being the perfect example to believers answered that question because He was also *born of a woman.* This is the main reason why John the Baptist refused to baptise Jesus (see Matthew 3), even when Jesus had told John to do so in order to fulfill all righteousness. Had John not baptised Jesus, He (Jesus) would not have been able to save man even though He had come as the Saviour.

Then cometh Jesus from Galilee to Jordan unto John, to be baptised of him. But John forbade him, saying, I have need to be baptised of thee, and comest thou to me? And Jesus answering said unto him, suffer it to be so now, for thus it becometh us to fulfill all righteousness. Then he suffered him. And Jesus, when he was baptised, went up straightway out of the water, and, lo, the heavens were opened unto him, and he saw the Spirit of God descending like a dove, and lighting upon him. And lo a voice from heaven, saying, this is my beloved Son, in whom I am well pleased. (Matthew 3:13-17)

Jesus answered and said unto him, verily, verily, I say unto thee, except a man be born again, he cannot see the kingdom of God. Nicodemus saith unto him, how can a man be born when he is old? Can he enter the second time into his mother's womb, and be born? Jesus answered, verily, verily, I say unto thee, except a man be born of water and of the Spirit, he cannot enter into the kingdom of God. That which is born of the flesh is flesh, and that which is born of the Spirit is spirit. Marvel not that I said unto thee, Ye must be born again. (John 3:3-7)

Many preachers and teachers of God's Word are pointing a finger at others, calling them 'Nicodemus', while they themselves are the spiritual 'Nicodemus' who are in the Church as leaders, and have not come to the knowledge of the *truth* that sets free. The revelation of how to be born again is shown by Jesus Christ to Nicodemus who was a ruler and a teacher of the Jews. The Bible states clearly that, he went to Jesus by night for some discussions, so Jesus told him, that except a man is born again, he cannot see or enter into the kingdom of God.

Nicodemus started his conversation with words of praise unto Jesus. Jesus told him that unless a man is born again, he could not see or enter into the kingdom of God. As the people of God who are going to give account of our stewardship to the Lord, we must learn not to be distracted by any praises of men because of the miracles they may see God doing through us. It is not the miracle that is important to God but the message behind the miracle, which is the *key* given by God to man for his salvation.

The first thing the Lord told Nicodemus (a teacher of the Jews) is that, *except a man is born again he cannot see the kingdom of God* (John 3:5)

The above statement or answer begged another question for Nicodemus who wanted to know more from this teacher, who came from God, since he was a teacher himself. Nicodemus, out of ignorance asking how a man can be born again when he is old, created another Key, this time entering into the Kingdom. There is a difference between seeing the Kingdom and entering into the Kingdom. Jesus answered him that except a man be born of water and of the Spirit, he cannot enter into the kingdom of God. He said, that which is born of the flesh is flesh and that which is born of the Spirit is spirit. The Bible is clear that every man born into this world is a seed of Adam and is born by flesh and blood. This is why Jesus tells Nicodemus that except a man is *born again* he cannot see or enter into the kingdom of God; although Nicodemus was a master or a teacher of the Jews, he had not received that revelation.

The Bible asks in the book of Job, how a man that is born of a woman, can be clean in the sight of God? (Job 25) This is the reason why when John the Baptist refused to baptise Jesus Christ, He told him to do so for the fulfillment of all righteousness, because Jesus Christ Himself was born of a woman. That made him the last Adam *(The Lord from heaven)* according to 1 Corinthians 15:45-47.

If a man is not *born again,* he cannot see or enter into the kingdom of God due to the veil of flesh on him. That is why on Calvary, when Jesus shouted and gave up the Ghost, the veil in the temple was torn in two allowing all to see the holy of holies. After the Lord was baptised by John the Baptist and came out from the water, the Holy Ghost descended upon Him and a voice from heaven confirmed Jesus as the son of the Father. That is what has paved the way for the sons and daughters of Adam and Eve, who are the images of God, to be born again into His kingdom as spiritual sons and daughters of God. This transformation from the image of God to a son of God means we, who are spiritual beings, have Jesus as our Father through the process of being born again. It does not matter how long we engage in prayer and fasting and alms giving, there is something that is required before one can see or enter into the kingdom of God (heaven).

There was a certain man in Caesarea called Cornelius, a centurion of the band called the Italian band. A devout man, and one that feared God with all his house, which gave much alms to the people, and prayed to God always. He saw in a vision evidently about the ninth hour of the day an angel of God coming in to him, and saying unto him, Cornelius. And when he looked on him, he was afraid, and said, what is it, Lord? And he said unto him, Thy prayers and thine alms are come up for a memorial before God. And now send men to Joppa, and call for one Simon, whose surname is Peter: He lodgeth with one Simon a tanner, whose house is by the seaside: he shall tell thee what thou oughtest to do ...While Peter yet spake these words, the Holy Ghost fell on all them which heard the word. And they of the circumcision, which believed, were astonished, as many as came with Peter, because that on the Gentiles also was poured out the gift of the Holy Ghost. For they heard them speak with tongues, and magnify God. Then answered Peter, Can any man forbid water, that these should not be baptised, which have received the Holy Ghost as well as we? And he commanded them to be baptised in the name of the Lord. Then prayed they him to tarry certain days. (Acts 10:1-6, 44-48)

We cannot change God's plan of salvation for us with other activities in the Church. He will still not save us. We must do things according to the pattern and the foundation shown to us by the early Apostles of Jesus Christ if we want to go to where they are; with their master, Jesus. It is only because of laziness that the Church is being tossed back and forth by every wind of doctrine. Some people do not go to Church with a Bible, and those who try to go with one do not even open it until the next Church activities. They depend only on what they hear from the pulpit.

(Now that he ascended, what is it but that he also descended first into the

lower parts of the earth? He that descended is the same also that ascended up far above all heavens, that he might fill all things.) And he gave some, apostles; and some, prophets; and some, evangelists; and some, pastors and teachers; For the perfecting of the saints, for the work of the ministry, for the edifying of the body of Christ: Till we all come in the unity of the faith, and of the knowledge of the Son of God, unto a perfect man, unto the measure of the stature of the fullness of Christ: That we henceforth be no more children, tossed to and fro, and carried about with every wind of doctrine, by the sleight of men, and cunning craftiness, whereby they lie in wait to deceive. (Ephesians 4:9-14)

Remember them, which have the rule over you, who have spoken unto you the word of God: whose faith follow, considering the end of their conversation. Jesus Christ the same yesterday, and today, and forever. Be not carried about with divers and strange doctrines. For it is a good thing that the heart be established with grace; not with meats, which have not profited them that have been occupied therein. (Hebrew 13:7-9)

It is one thing to own a Bible and close it and put it under your pillow, and it is another thing to open it and search the Scriptures for your salvation. It is time to rise up and search from the Bible for genuine salvation, which starts with *repentance* and *baptism* by the Apostles of old. If Nicodemus who was a Jew and a leader of the Jewish religion, needed to be born again of water and of the Spirit before he could see or enter into the kingdom of God, then what about us, the Gentiles, who are idol worshipers?

As you read on, may the Lord give you the understanding of why Nicodemus who was a man and a teacher, needed to be *born again* before he could see or enter into the kingdom of God.

May God bless you as you do so. Amen!

CHAPTER ONE

Religious Culture

The increase in idol worship in the world these days is a result of a religious culture. The spirit behind this is growing very fast and has now entered into the Church. If we do not identify and resist these cultures, they will do more harm than good to many Christians; making them think, they are worshiping the one true God while serving Satan and his human agents.

Our own confession of being a member of a particular Church testifies against us, that we are bound by religious and denominational cords, which separate one Church from another. This was the spirit that entered into the Church of Corinth during the days of Apostle Paul. Some believers said they were of Cephas while some said they were of Apollos. Others yet said they were of Paul, and some even said they were of Jesus .((1 Cornthians 1:10)

Satan is not doing any new thing in the Church, but only repeating his old system of deception. In the time of Moses, he created division through Korah, Dathan and Abiram, who died with their followers in the wilderness. (Numbers 10:11-15)

The same spirit continued to follow the people of God after the death of Moses. When Joshua was chosen by God to lead His people, Joshua told the people, *"choose you this day whom you will worship, the God of your fathers or the other gods"* (Joshua 24:15) because of their murmuring. God always uses one leader to lead His chosen people. The declaration that we are a follower of *this* man of God, or the founder of *this* church or *that* church, is proof that many believers have become followers of men rather than God. Today we have many founders of Churches who are not connected to, or built upon the Apostlic foundation of Jesus Christ being the chief corner stone.

Apostle Paul, by revelation, said God, the Spirit was in Christ; the anointed body, known as the Son, reconciling men back unto Himself. (2 Corinthians 5:18) If I continue Apostle Paul's revelation, I would say Christ is reconciling man unto Himself until the rapture. Let us look carefully at the following Scriptures.

Now I beseech you, brethren, by the name of our Lord Jesus Christ, that ye all speak the same thing, and that there be no divisions among you, but that ye be perfectly joined together in the same mind and in the same judgment. For it hath been declared unto me of you, my brethren, by them which are of the house of Chloe, that there are contentions among you. Now this I say, that every one of you saith, I am of Paul, and I of Apollos, and I of Cephas, and I of Christ. Is Christ divided? Was Paul crucified for you? Or were ye baptised in the name of Paul? (1 Corinthians 1:10-12)

Now therefore ye are no more strangers and foreigners, but fellow citizens with the saints, and of the household of God. And are build upon the foundation of the Apostles and Prophets, Jesus Christ himself being the chief corner stone. In whom all the building fitly framed together growth unto a Holy temple in the Lord. In whom ye also are builded together for a habitation of God through the Spirit. (Ephesians 2:19-21)

According to Solomon, the writer of the book of Ecclesiastes, *to everything there is a season and a time to every purpose under the heaven.* (Ecclesiastes 3:1) The facts about the above statement cannot be changed by man.

There are things that come out in their season and then end or go when the season ends. There is much research going on under the heaven concerning the truth about God's Word. If it is not the season, God will not give the revelation.

From much research of baptisms in the Bible, God, for His own reasons, has given some scholars the revelation to write about baptism in Jesus' name. Baptism is only mentioned in connection with the New Testament church, specifically to wash away the transgressions of sinners and in so doing, making them righteous before God.

The purpose of this book is to open your understanding unto some hidden mysteries about baptism such as: what is baptism? Why do I need to be baptised? Who ordained baptism? And what Jesus said about baptism?

Behind every deception stands the father of all lies, Satan. This is why the Lord said you *shall know the Truth and the Truth shall make you free.* (John 8:32) For some people, this Scripture is misunderstood, but if you can receive the *Truth* that sets free, which is in the knowledge of who Jesus is, *the Way, the Truth and the Life*, (John 14:6) then you have made the right choice.

This book will serve to awaken Christians in the area of baptism through the knowledge and understanding of who Jesus is, and what He told His disciples to do that makes it different from all other religions and gives us the name, Christians.

As you read on, the Lord will give you deeper understanding that you may never have come across since you have been studying your Bible. It takes commitment or dedication. Remember the Ethiopian eunuch who was reading the Scriptures without understanding until the Lord sent Philip to meet him in the desert. God is not an author of confusion, in contrast, He is sharing His joy in the hearts of people by giving them the truth, and so, have your share as you read on.

And the angel of the Lord spake unto Philip saying, Arise, and go toward the south unto the way that goeth down from Jerusalem unto Gaza, which is desert. [27]And he rose and went and behold, a man of Ethiopia, an eunuch of great authority under Candace queen of the Ethiopians, who had the charge of all her treasure, and had come to Jerusalem for to worship. [28]Was returning, and sitting in his chariot read Esaias the prophet. [29]Then the Spirit said unto Philip, go near, and join thyself to this chariot. [30]And Philip ran thither to him and heard him read the prophet Esaias, and said, understandest thou that thou readest? [31]And he said, how can I except some man should guide me? And he desired Philip that he would come up and sit with him.

... [37]And Philip said, if thou believest with all thine heart, thou mayest. And he answered and said, I believe that Jesus Christ is the Son of God. [38]And he

commanded the chariot to stand still, and they went down both into the water, both Philip and the Eunuch, and he baptised him. [39] And when they were come up out of the water, the Spirit of the Lord caught away Philip, that the Eunuch saw him no more, and he went on his way rejoicing. (Acts 8:26-31, 37-39.)

The body of Christ seems to be incomplete. The reason is very simple: almost all the people of God everywhere are fasting and praying for power to do signs and wonders. Only a small proportion are praying for God's direction in the Kingdom's work. Today, we hear of more prophets than evangelist or teachers in the Church of God. We forget that Jesus Christ was a great teacher to His disciples whom He instructed and commanded to go into the world to preach to all nations.

What happened between the Ethiopian eunuch and Philip is a great example to those who want to understand the Scriptures. The Bible makes it clear that the Ethiopian eunuch was reading a Scripture fulfilled through Jesus from the book of Isaiah but he could not see the truth until God sent Philip to meet him in the wilderness to ask him if he understood what he had read.

The Lord said, *ask and it shall be given unto you.* (Matthew 7:7) I believe that, had the Ethiopian eunuch had told Philip that he understood the Scripture, Philip would not have troubled himself to teach him.

Today, many are reading the Bible and studying it all alone without any spiritual understanding, yet they refuse to be taught because they do not want to humble themselves to anyone since the Lord is using them for one thing or the other in His vineyard. Many forget that God by His grace can still call someone who does not understand His Word, or know the truth. Since they have faith in the name of Jesus Christ, such believers can still accomplish great works in God. Many Christians have forgotten that in spite of the devil's deception, God still pronounced His judgment on Adam and Eve for their disobedient in the Garden of Eden. Since the Word of God is alive and creative, it does that which is written. It not only judges whoever may lead you to disobedience but also judges you whether you obey or disobey.

There is a way we answer questions to our own destruction, which might not be biblical. This is why the Bible says, *there is a way that seemed right in the sight of a man but the end thereof is destruction.* (Proverbs 14:12) If the topic of baptism is raised in a Churchi t brings up many questions. What is baptism? Do I need to be baptised before I can be saved? What about the thief of the cross, did he get baptised? If I preach the gospel to somebody who receives the Word with repentance, but could not be baptised before he died, can he be saved?

In fact, there are numerous questions people ask to their own destruction. The question, do I need to be baptised before I can be saved, is still being asked by many today when it comes to the teachings on baptism.

Many pastors and teachers of God's Word tell their members or listeners that baptism does not save. They keep on teaching that all one needs is faith in the finished work of the Calvary cross on which Jesus Christ died to save all sinners. Some teach their flock that baptism is optional; that all that is needed for your salvation is to confess Jesus Christ as your personal saviour and believe in your heart that He is the son of God. They mostly support this teachings with the Word of God twisted to their own destruction.

Please let us read from the Scriptures and see how the devil has corrupted the salvation message.

That if thou shall confess with thy mouth the Lord Jesus and shall believe in thine heart that God hath raised him from the dead, thou shall be saved. For with the heart man believeth unto righteousness and with the mouth, confession is made unto salvation. (Romans10:9-10)

The above Scripture does not separate baptism from salvation, but confirms that the name of the Lord is to be used for salvation, and that name should be called upon during baptism. Since *all have sinned and come short of the glory of God,* (Romans 3:23) we need remission or our sins through the blood of Jesus Christ who was crucified for our sake.

Apostle Paul, after saying that whosoever shall call upon the name of the Lord shall be saved, continues by asking the Romans *how then they shall call*

on him in whom they have not believed. And how shall they believe in him of whom they have not heard? And how shall they hear without a preacher? And how shall they preach except they are sent? (Romans 10: 14-15)
As a wise master-builder, Paul was building upon the Apostle's foundation one step at a time, so that Christians could understand him better. Let us read the following Scriptures for more understanding.

[19]Now therefore ye are no more strangers and foreigners, but fellow citizens with the saints, and of the household of God. [20]And are build upon the foundation of the Apostles and the Prophets, Jesus Christ himself being the chief corner stone. [21]In whom all the building fitly framed together growth unto an holy temple in the Lord. [22]In whom ye also are builded together for an habitation of God through the Spirit. (Ephesians 2:19-22)

[9]For we are labourers together with God, ye are God's husbandry, ye are God's building. [10]According to the grace of God which is given me, as a wise master builder, I have laid the foundation and another buildeth there on, but let every man take heed how he buildeth thereupon. [11]For other foundation can no man lay than that is laid, which is Jesus Christ. (1Corinthians 3:9-11)

When Paul wrote to the Ephesians, he mentioned the Apostles' and the Prophets' foundation, which had already been laid by Apostle Peter, the Apostle to whom the Lord gave the *keys of the Kingdom*. When Paul was talking to the church in Corinth, he said he had laid the foundation. This should not confuse you because Paul was referring to the church in Corinth at that time, since the people wanted to change the foundation laid down through Apostle Peter's revelation.

The Lord Jesus Christ told Nicodemus that *except a man is born of water and of the Spirit he cannot enter into the kingdom of God*. No chosen man of God has ever diverted from what Jesus told Nicodemus, they all did according to Jesus' Word. The Apostle concluded that the elect or the Christians have *one Lord, one baptism and one faith.* (Ephesians 4:5)

[4]There is one body, and one Spirit even as ye are called in one hope of your calling, [5]One Lord, one faith, one baptism, [6]one God and Father of all, who is above all, and through all and in you all. (Ephesians 4:4-6)

Apostle Paul's Perception of Baptism

And it came to pass, that, while Apollos was at Corinth, Paul having passed through the upper coasts came to Ephesus and finding certain disciples, He said unto them, have ye received the Holy Ghost since ye believed? And they said unto him, we have not so much as heard whether there be any Holy Ghost. And he said unto them, unto what then were, ye baptised? And they said, unto John's baptism, then said Paul, John verily baptised with the baptism of repentance, saying, unto the people, that they should believe on him which should come after him, that is, on Christ Jesus. When they heard thus, they were baptised in the name of the Lord Jesus. And when Paul had laid his hands upon them, the Holy Ghost came on them, and they spake with tongues, and prophesied. And all the men were about twelve. (Acts 19:1-7)

From the above Scripture, Paul gives the true interpretation of baptism. With humility and obedience to his instructions, all whom Paul met were baptised in the name of Jesus Christ for the remission of their sins. They all received the Holy Ghost immediately as Paul laid his hands on them, and started speaking in tongues and prophesying. They lacked knowledge of the Word of God in relation to baptism, but when they heard the true Word, they received it with joy instead of arguing with Paul.

We will only have ourselves to blame if we lose our lives through fighting against the truth instead of embracing it. No matter how we justify our blindness through Scripture, the truth cannot be changed. We do so to our own destruction and that of our followers. Apostle Paul told his son in the Lord, Timothy, *"take heed unto thyself and to the doctrine"*, and by so doing he will save himself and his followers. (1 Timothy 4:16)

There is no two ways to heaven. The Lord taught His disciples in Matthew 7 of the *narrow and the broad way*, and ended up talking about the false prophets. You take either the narrow way to heaven or the broad way to hell. So be careful which way you choose.

The Apostle's statement of *whosoever shall call upon the name of the Lord shall be saved* (Romans 10:13), is not telling the Church that baptism is eliminated from the salvation plan of God. It is the confirmation of Peter's word that baptism saves. The name of the Lord is called upon for salvation during baptism, to fulfill the Word of Jesus Christ to Nicodemus that unless a man be born again with water and of the Spirit, he cannot see or enter into the kingdom of God.

CHAPTER TWO

Born of Water and of the Spirit

Which sometime were disobedient, when once the longsuffering of God waited in the days of Noah, while the ark was a preparing, wherein few, that is, eight souls were saved by water. The like figure where unto even, baptism doth also now save us (not the putting away of the filth of the flesh, but the answer of a good conscience toward God) by the resurrection of Jesus Christ. (1 Peter 3:20-21)

Our God is a loving father who is not willing that any soul should perish. For this; He gave to His church, Pastors who could lead them in the knowledge of the Word of God so as to do away with the devil's deceit.

The Lord spoke in parables to reveal many truths to His chosen servants, whom He commissioned to, teach and lead His people through the *narrow way*; the knowledge of who Jesus is. The understanding of His Word is what will separate the elect from the religious ones

And I will give you pastors according to mine heart, which shall feed you with knowledge and understanding. (Jeremiah 3:15)

My sheep hear my voice and I know them, and they follow me, and I give unto them eternal life, and they shall never perish neither shall any man pluck them out of my hand. (John 10:27-28)

Water has been part of God's plan of salvation from the very beginning. When Jesus told Nicodemus that man needs to be born of water and of the Spirit before he can enter the Kingdom, He was not diverting from His plan of saving His people. The only difference now is that we are to be born again with water and of the Spirit into the kingdom of God, and baptism signifies salvation.

To be born again *with water* and *of the Spirit* is to be baptised in water in the name of Jesus Christ and receive the Holy Spirit with the gift of speaking in tongues. If a man repents and is baptised in Jesus' name for the remission of his sin, he puts on Christ. If he is baptised by the Holy Spirit, Jesus comes to dwell in him. So he becomes like Jesus Christ. The Bible says we *shall be like Him when He appears*. (1 John 3:2) It is not your position in the Church that will make you to *be like Him*, but putting on Christ *(garment of righteousness),* and receiving the Holy Spirit as the hope of glory *Christ in me the hope of glory, (Colossians 1:27)* and living in holiness.

You may have all the privileges but do not let your position deceive you. If you have never *put on Christ* by being baptised in His name for the remission of your sin, now is the accepted time. Right now is the day of your salvation; delay can be dangerous There is a question behind our salvation. Apostle Paul asked the disciples of John the Baptist whether they had received the Holy Spirit since they believed, and into what baptism they had been baptised. It is in obedience to Jesus' command to be born of water and of the Spirit.

If you have not fulfilled this, do not be deceived. Rise up, and find someone who understands this doctrine, and allow yourself to be baptised in Jesus' name for the remission of your sin.

Read the following Scriptures for more understanding, because in this dispensation, God is not doing it like in the days of Joshua the high priest.

And he showed me Joshua the high priest standing before the angel of the Lord, and Satan standing at his right hand to resist him. [2]And the Lord said unto Satan. The Lord rebuke thee, O Satan, even the Lord that hath chosen Jerusalem rebuke thee; is not this a brand plucked out of the fire? [3]Now Joshua was clothed with filthy garments, and stood before the angel. And he answered and spoke. Unto those that stood before him, saying, take away the filthy garments from him, and unto him he said behold, I have caused thine iniquity to pass from thee, and I will clothe thee with change of raiment. (Zechariah. 3:1-5)

Then they that gladly received his word were baptised; and the same day there were added unto them about three thousand souls. And they continued steadfastly in the apostle's doctrine and fellowship, and in breaking of bread and in prayers. (Acts 2:41-42)

The truth about God's Word is the only thing that can save a sinner. Today in the Church, the devil has succeeded in labeling deception with what people call, the truth. We have people with voices like an earthquake, yet God is not in them. Some speak like thunder and fire in the Church but God is not in them. God is still speaking to His children with the small still voice, and only the chosen can recognise His voice. It is not that a preacher jumps and shouts that makes him or her anointed with the Holy Spirit, but their knowledge of the Word of God, and the ability and grace to interpret it appropriately to the people of God to win their souls for Christ.

In these last days, many men of God base their success in ministry on worldly attributes and achievements such as the size of their buildings, the number of congregation members, books they have written (many not ordained by God), and church titles such as Bishop, Psalmist, Master , and even Prophet and Apostle. This is often why those with only few members yet with greater anointing are not recognised by man, but Jesus Christ who called them, knows them. In short, this act is a deception from the devil.

I am not saying that having a large building and membership is necessarily a bad thing, but rather look at what Jesus told the woman at the well.

But the hour cometh, and now is, when the true worshippers shall worship the father in Spirit and in truth; for the Father seeketh such to worship him. God is a Spirit and they that worship him must worship him in Spirit and in truth. The woman saith unto him, I know that Messiah cometh, which is called Christ; when he is come, he will tell us all things. Jesus saith unto her, I that speak unto thee am he. (John 4:23-26)

From the above conversation between the Samaritan woman and Jesus Christ, we know how to trace the true church of Jesus Christ in the midst of deceivers who have turned the sufferings of the Calvary cross into covetousness and personal gain. The Lord Jesus spoke of two things, the Spirit and the Truth, as the sign of true worship, since He is the owner of the true Church. The Lord did not leave His church to be deceived by false prophets and teachers who are turning the Word of God upside down. Matthew 24 talks about, the deceivers of these last days who will use *signs and wonders* to draw people after them, but they cannot deceive the elect.

Fom the beginning, the Lord has made it impossible for them to deceive the elect.

For there shall arise false Christ's, and false prophets, and shall show great signs and wonders, insomuch that, if it were possible, they shall deceive the very elect. (Matthew 24:24)

Even the Spirit of truth whom the world cannot receive, because it seeth him not, neither knoweth him, but ye know him, for he dwelleth with you, and shall be in you. I will not leave you comfortless I will come to you. (John 14:17)

The Lord gave us the *Sword of Victory*, before His crucifixion. He told the Samaritan woman that true worshippers [would] worship the Father in spirit and in truth. Jesus Christ kept on teaching and talking about the Father until Philip asked Him to show them the Father.

Philip saith unto him, Lord shows us the father, and it sufficeth us. Jesus saith unto him. Have I been so long time with you, and yet hast thou not known me, Philip? He that hath seen me hath seen the Father and how sayest thou then, shew us the Father? (John 14:8-9)

Forasmuch then as the children are partakers of flesh and blood he also himself likewise took part of the same, that through death he might destroy him that had the power of death, that is the devil. And deliver them who through fear of death were all their lifetime subject to bondage. For verily he took not on him the nature of angels, but he took on him the seed of Abraham. (Hebrews 2:14-16)

The Lord Jesus Christ told His disciples that He will build His church *and the gates of hell shall never prevail against it.* (Matthew 16:18) Jesus is the founder and the father of His own church, therefore, false doctrine can never prevail against it.

When Jacob dreamed about a ladder set up on earth; the top reaching heaven, and angels of God ascending and descending, he awoke and said, *surely the Lord is in this place and I knew not. He was afraid and said ... this is none other place but the house of God, and this is the gate of heaven.* (Genesis 28:17)

If heaven and hell have gates, as alluded to in this Scripture, then we must search the Scriptures, and ask for God's mercy and grace so that He will show us the gate by which we need to enter. We, and our followers, must not be deceived into believing we are candidates for heaven, while we may well end up in hell.

In Matthew 7 Jesus Christ gives the essential teaching on the narrow and the broad way. He ends up talking about false prophets, and also about the judgment day when people will say they did this and did that, and even cast out demons in His name but He will tell them to go away as He does not know them. The truth about Christianity and salvation is not how anointed you claim to be or how many years you have been in the faith.

Many measure their salvation with the miracles they do and some even measure theirs with the size of their congregation. Such things may be good but all we need to know and understand is that salvation itself is a gift. Those who profess Christianity without this gift of salvation will continue to persecute those who have been gifted with salvation *(the Truth)* until the rapture.

For by grace are ye saved through faith, and that not of yourselves, it is the gift of God. Not of works, lest any man should boast. For we are his workmanship, created in Christ Jesus unto good works, which God hath before ordained that we should walk in them. (Ephesians 2:8-10)

As Bible-believing Christians, we need to pray for God's mercy that will lead us into His saving grace. It is not the amount of research we undertake that matters, but His mercy and grace that saves. The Lord told Apostle Paul, that *my grace is sufficient for you.* (2 Corinthians 12:9) It is God's mercy that will lead us into His saving grace where the *rock* of salvation is. Jesus told the people of His time that many will struggle to enter into the kingdom of God but cannot.

If the Lord does not show you mercy you can only pass through the *broad way* that leads to destruction This is exactly what is happening in the Church today: people are missing their way. The rock on which Moses was placed for salvation is Jesus Christ *(God Himself),* and He followed His people from Egypt to the promised land. (see Exodus 33:21)

Moreover brethren I would not that ye should be ignorant, how that all our Fathers were under the cloud, and all passed through the sea, and were all baptised unto Moses in the cloud and in the sea. And did all eat the same spiritual meat, and did all drink the same spiritual drink for they drank of that spiritual Rock that followed them and that Rock was Christ. (1 Corinthians 10:1-4)

Moses was the deliverance minister the Lord used for the Jews in Egypt. This is why the Bible says the people *(the Hebrew fathers)* were baptised unto him through the sea and in the cloud. (see Hebrews 11) The law also came through him.

From the above Scripture, we see that the rock played a vital part int the salvation of the Jews. Let us come to the conclusion of the whole matter of born of water and of the Spirit.

How then can man be justified with God? Or how can he be clean that is born of a woman? Behold even to the moon, and it shineth not, yea, the stars are not pure in his sight. How much less man, that is a worm? And the son of man, which is a worm? (Job 25:4-6)

Then cometh Jesus from Galilee to Jordan unto John, to be baptised of him. But John forbade him, saying, I have need to be baptised of thee, and comest thou to me? And Jesus answering said unto him, suffer it to be so now, for thus it becometh us to fulfill all righteousness. Then he suffered him. And Jesus, when he was baptised, went up straightway out of the water, and, lo, the heavens were opened unto him, and he saw the Spirit of God descending like a dove, and lighting upon him. And lo a voice from heaven, saying, This is my beloved Son, in whom I am well pleased. (Matthew 3:13-17)

If Jesus Christ whom Apostle Paul referred to as the *Lord from heaven,* had to be baptised in water to fulfill all righteousness, because he was born of a woman, then why do some so-called men of God of today tell their followers that one can enter heaven without being baptised? This is far from the truth. Most of them use the *thief on the cross* (see Luke 23) as an example to deceive themselves and others.

Remember, you cannot change the Word of God. Jesus said unless a man is born of water and of the Spirit, he cannot see or enter into the kingdom of

God. This is what the Lord Jesus Christ wants His servants to teach His followers who want to come to be with Him in His kingdom.

John baptised the people for repentance, but Jesus Christ was baptised for the fulfillment of all righteousness because he was born of a woman. This makes the baptism of Jesus Christ different from all others. The thief on the cross was saved before the establishment of God's church here on earth.

After Calvary, God now saves man through His Church. Apostle Paul says: *... For though ye have ten thousand instructors in Christ, yet have ye not many fathers: for in Christ Jesus I have begotten you through the gospel. Wherefore I beseech you, be ye followers of me.* (1 Corinthians 4:15-16)

CHAPTER THREE

The Sons of God in Heaven

Now there was a day when the sons of God came to present themselves before the Lord, and Satan came also among them. And the Lord said unto Satan, whence camest thou? Then Satan answered the Lord, and said, from going to and fro in the earth, and from walking up and down in it. And the Lord said unto Satan, hast thou considered my servant Job, that there is none like him in the earth, a perfect and an upright man, one that feareth God, and eschewed evil. (Job 1:6-8)

The Bible says, in the *beginning, God created the heavens and the earth.* (Genesis 1:1) It goes on to say heaven is the dwelling place of the Lord while the earth is His footprint. From Job 1:6-8 above, we are told that there was a day when the sons of God came to present themselves before the Lord, and Satan came with them. God asked him where was he coming from and has he noticed His servant Job that there is none like him on earth. This conversation between God and the devil in heaven concerning Job gives us an understanding of the *sons of God* whose dwelling is in heaven and the *sons of man*, whose dwelling is on earth.

Job was on earth while Satan was negotiating his destruction with God in heaven. The Bible makes it evident that God is a Spirit, and, if God is a Spirit, His sons that went to present themselves unto Him are also spirits whose dwelling is in heaven. God and Satan were in heaven during the discussion, while Job was on the earth not knowing what was going on concerning him. This highlights the reality of the sons of God, spiritual beings whose dwelling is in heaven, and the sons of men whose dwelling is here on earth. Having the understanding that there is a vast difference between the sons of God whose dwelling is in heaven (spiritual beings) and the sons of men whose dwelling is on the earth (physical beings), will help us to understand this scriptural passage that says:

And God said, let us make man in our image, after our likeness, and let them have dominion over the fish of the Sea, and over the fowl of the air, and over the cattle and over all the earth, and over every creeping thing that creepeth upon the earth. So God created man in his own image, in the image of God created him, male and female created he them. (Genesis 1:26-27)

Many denominations or religious sects affirm their belief in the Trinity that teaches God in three persons: *the Father, Son and Holy Ghost,* with the above Scripture. When creating man, these three persons of the Trinity, communicated and agreed to create man in their own image as body, soul and spirit.

This is the doctrine of the spirit of the antichrist; because it is contrary to the Jewish belief of *hear oh! Israel the Lord our God is one Lord,*(Deuteronomy 6:4) and the Christian *(the spiritual Jews)* belief that *we have but one God.* (Mark 12:32)

Jesus Christ and His Apostles have made the matter clear to stop us from being confused. Jesus said God is a Spirit and Holy by nature. (John 14:17) Apostle Paul also said God-the Eternal Spirit and the Father of all creations manifested Himself in flesh in the person of Jesus Christ. (1 Timothy 3:16)

With this understanding, there should not be any argument among the children of God about the image of God that is in man. This is His spirit: the-*Breath*, which He breathed into the nostril of man that transformed him from clay into a living soul. The same thing is what happens during the new birth. God pours His spirit into man's dead spirit for a transformation from a living soul into a living spirit known as the regeneration.

The *sons of God* that Job mentions, are the spiritual beings that God created to worship Him, whose dwelling is in the heavens. The sons of God were the main cause of the flood when God destroyed the world and saved Noah and his household.

And it came to pass when men began to multiply on the face of the earth, and daughters were born unto them, that the sons of God saw the daughters of men that they were fair, and they took them wives of all which they chose. And the Lord said, my spirit shall not always strive with man, for that he also is flesh, yet his days shall be an hundred and twenty years. There were giants in the earth in those days, and also after that, when the sons of God came in unto the daughters of men, and they bare children to them, the same became mighty men which were of old, men of renown. And God saw that the wickedness of man was great in the earth, and that every imagination of the thoughts of his heart was only evil continually. And it repented the Lord that he had made man on the earth, and it grieved him at his heart. And the Lord said, I will destroy man whom I have created from the face of the earth, both man, and beast, and the creeping thing, and the fowls of the air, for it repented me that I have made them. But Noah found grace in the eyes of the Lord. (Genesis 6:1-8)

Be not forgetful to entertain strangers, for thereby some have <u>entertained angels unawares</u>. (Hebrews 13:2 underlining mine)

The Bible makes it clear that when men began to multiply on earth, and daughters were born, the sons of God saw that the daughters of men were beautiful, and they married them and gave birth to giants and mighty men of mixed nature. This increased the evil that led God to destroy them and the earth with a flood.

Hebrews 13:2 gives us the understanding of how the sons of God took the daughters of men as wives through entertainment. They had angels *(the sons of God)* who visited them and they entertain them, not knowing that they were angels in the human form.

If the Bible says the sons of God saw that the daughters of men whose dwelling is in the flesh and are on the earth, were beautiful, and came down to marry them, it means the spiritual beings who are angels came in a human form. We need to understand that the *sons of God* were created beings. The Bible makes it plain that in the beginning God *created the heaven and the earth and everything that is in them.* (Genesis 1:1)

The Sons of God on Earth

He was in the world and the world was made by him, and the world knew him not, He came unto his own, and his own received him not. But as many as received him, to them gave he power to become the sons of God, even to them that believe on his name. Which were born, not of blood, nor of the will of man, but of God. And the Word was made flesh, and dwelt among us, (and we beheld his glory, the glory as of the only begotten of the Father) full of grace and truth. (John 1:10-14)

For as much then as the children are partakers of flesh and blood, he also himself likewise took part of the same, that through death he might destroy him that had the power of death that is, the devil. And deliver them who through fear of death were all their lifetime subject to bondage. For verily he took not on him the nature of angels, but he took on him the seed of Abraham. (Hebrews 2:14-16)

There is a clear difference between the children of God *(the sons of God),* and the image of God here on earth. Because the Bible states that, in the beginning God made man in His own image and not His son. According to the Scriptures, God created the world and everything by His Word, but man was created from the earth; of the ground, and God breathed the breath of life into his nostril and man became a living soul. (see Genesis 1-2)

Every human being on earth belongs to God, although Satan and his demons may at times put on flesh and walk among us as human beings. Since God is the father of all spirits; let us leave it to Him to separate the weed from the crop while we seek His grace to understand these studies, so that we might be saved.

The Bible says in *John 1:14* that, *the Word became flesh* and this forms the basis of our studies. If we do not understand the reason and purpose the Word became flesh, we will continue deceiving others and ourselves with our own imaginations. The books of John and Hebrews are very helpful in the understanding of the deep things of the Word, which *became flesh and dwelt among us.*

The above Scriptures make it clear that the children of God here on earth are partakers of flesh and blood. God cannot contradict His Word because He is the Word Himself. He told Adam and Eve to replenish the earth and, if He creates another human being apart from the descendants of Adam and Eve, it would be a contradiction. Such confusion would then be just like the sons of God from heaven who married the daughters of men who then bore strange beings whose evil and wickedness caused the flood.

For Him to give birth to His own sons on earth, God broke the circle of replenishment of the first Adam by becoming the second Adam. He came down from heaven in order to bring about the birth to His sons, because children are born and not created. This is why Jesus told Nicodemus, that except a man *(image of God and the son of Adam)* be born again he cannot see or enter into the kingdom of God.

It takes the New Birth to become a son or daughter of God (Jesus Christ). This is done through the gospel of Jesus Christ. He has paid the price for our sins, taken on the curse and suffered the death, which we inherited through Adam and Eve when they went against the instruction of God in the Garden of Eden. For the descendants of Adam and Eve to be free (sinless), someone must first open these three gates so that man can come out, one-step at a time, into total freedom from sin, curse and death.

Freedom from Sin

The Bible says: *all have sin and have come short of the glory of God.* (Romans 3:23) The blood of Jesus Christ was shed for the sins committed by Adam and Eve that we inherited. Our sins are washed away through baptism in Jesus' name after repentance and acceptance of Jesus Christ as our personal Lord and Saviour.

Freedom from the Curse

The cross plays a vital role in eradicating the curse pronounced upon man, and not the curse pronounced upon the earth. The earth will continue to struggle with the curse. Jesus said, *"I have overcome the world, so in me you will have peace, but in the world you will have tribulation." (John 16:33)*

Jesus Christ was nailed to the cross because of the curse pronounced on man and He, likewise, nailed the curse on the cross. So in processing our salvation, He was judged for our sins and His Father (The Holy Spirit) left His body. This caused Him to cry out, *"my Father, my Father why have thou forsaken me?"* (Mark 15:34)

After this, His dead body was taken down from the cross and buried in a tomb, and since there was no sin or curse found on the body, it became the Christ (The anointed body) so the Holy Spirit (the Father) could now enter into the body again and cause it to resurrect. This now paves the way for whosoever may wish to be born again of water and of the Spirit, according to the reply He gave Nicodemus.

Freedom from Death

If Jesus Christ did not rise from the dead, man would be hopelessly condemned to perish in hell forever. The third and final stage of our salvation is the resurrection. This is when a child of God receives the Holy Spirit into their dead spirit with the evidence of speaking in tongues.

There are so many Christians bound by false doctrine; claiming to be sons and daughters of God. They have not passed through the born again process in the name of Jesus. Man (Adam) was sent away from God because of his disobedience. Adam went from sin to curse and then from curse to death. Jesus Christ, the saviour of man (the second Adam) came to pay the price of our salvation, through obedience to death on the cross and then resurrection from death.

The Call to Salvation

And he (Ananias) said, the God of our fathers hath chosen thee, that thou shouldest know his will, and see that just one, and shouldest hear the voice of his mouth. For thou shall be his wittness unto all men of what thou hast seen and heard. And now why tarriest thou? Arise, and be baptised, and wash away thy sins, calling on the name the Lord. (Acts 22:14-16)

If only the children of God would allow the Holy Spirit to interpret the Scriptures to them, the devil and his agents would not operate successfully in the church of God. If we use our carnal mind to interpret or complete some uncompleted statement that we may come across in the Bible, we complete it to our own destruction. The Word of God must not be taken lightly because it is life and death.

From the above Scriptures, we see that Apostle Paul, who wrote to the Romans, was baptised; calling on the name of the Lord. As a sinner, saved by God's grace, he needed his sins to be washed away by the blood of Jesus. This is only achieved through baptism in Jesus' name, because all have sin and come short of the glory of God. Paul was called to salvation through the blood that Jesus shed on the cross of Calvary, which washes away all sin.

Let us read the following Scripture for more understanding.

For whosoever shall call upon the name of the Lord shall be saved. How then shall they call on him in whom they have not believed? And how shall they believe in him of whom they have not heard? And how shall they hear without a preacher? And how shall they preach, except they be sent? As it is written, How beautiful are the feet of them that preach the gospel of peace, and bring glad tidings of good things! But they have not all obeyed the gospel. For Esaias saith, Lord, who hath believed our report? So then faith cometh by hearing, and hearing by the word of God. (Romans 10:13-17)

Every Christian knows that the Lord Jesus Christ called the twelve disciples and commissioned them to go into the world and preach the gospel unto all nations. He also instructed them to baptise all those who believe, for the remission of their sins, and to receive the Holy Spirit for salvation. The apostles were commanded to teach this to the Church.

Apostle Paul's statement of whosoever shall call upon the *name* of the Lord shall be saved, must be well understood before we start leading the people of God astray with the doctrine of our own imagination. The Apostle has already written to the Church in Corinth that, *no other foundation can a man lay apart from that which is laid that is Jesus Christ.* (1 Corinthians 3:11) Since we are commanded to study the Word, let us trace from the Bible, the *foundation,* which the chosen Apostle (Apostle Peter) of Jesus Christ laid for our salvation.

Now when they heard this, they were pricked in their heart, and said unto Peter and to the rest of the apostles, Men and brethren, what shall we do? Then Peter said unto them, Repent, and be baptised every one of you in the name of Jesus Christ for the remission of sins, and ye shall receive the gift of the Holy Ghost. For the promise is unto you, and to your children, and to all that are afar off, even as many as the Lord our God shall call. And with many other words did he testify and exhort, saying, save yourselves from this untoward generation. (Acts 2:37-40)

The Lord commanded His disciples to go into the world to preach the gospel and baptise those who will believe, and teach them everything that He commanded them for salvation. Remember, the Church was established before the calling of Apostle Paul who was a persecutor of the established truth. The New Testament Church was established on the foundations of belief, repentance and baptism in Jesus' name for the remission of sins and the receiving of the Holy Spirit.

A believer of the gospel must be baptised to fulfill God's plan of salvation for His people. When John the Baptist refused to baptise the Lord Jesus Christ, He told John to do so to fulfill all righteousness. The Lord did so to show us that no one is exempted from baptism, and it takes one to baptise one, because no one can baptise himself insomuch as no dead man can bury himself or no one can give birth to himself.

Just as Jesus said, *"that day many shall say unto me in your name, we cast out the devil and healed the sick but I will say unto them I know you not"* (Matthew 7:22), many people who read the Bible without looking for teachers will tell the Lord on that day that they were deceived by Apostle Paul. This excuse will not be accepted. Apostle Peter had already written that, by the wisdom given unto Paul, he has written some *things which those who are unlearned and unstable wrest, as they do with the other scriptures, unto their own destruction* (2 Peter 3:16), simply because those things are hard to be understood without a teacher.

Many Christians believe themselves to be too anointed to look for a teacher. They believe they have been anointed to do great works in the kingdom of God. Being made great by God, Himself, who can teach them anything else? Apostle Peter has made the matter clear to us, concerning the writings of the Apostle Paul, chosen by Jesus Christ for us Gentiles. To understand the Apostle Paul's letters to the church you need to learn. Every student needs a teacher who is able to teach to his or her understanding. In his letter to the Romans, Apostle Paul says some have been given the gift of teaching. (1 Corinthians 12:28)

Let us look closely at the Bible passage the enemy is using to eliminate the teaching ministry from the church of God today.

These things have I written unto you concerning them that seduce you. But the anointing which ye have received of him abideth in you, and ye need not that any man teach you, but as the same anointing teacheth you of all things, and is truth, and is no lie, and even as it hath taught you, ye shall abide in him. (1 John 2:26-27)

Satan's ministry within the church of Jesus Christ is to misinterpret the Scriptures, with the aim of dragging God's children to hell, since he is already destined for destruction. But God, by His grace, has made it impossible for him to corrupt those who are chosen by Him. That is why; Jesus told His followers in Matthew 24:22 that, for the sake of the elect, the Lord will cut the days, if not, no flesh shall be saved.

God has already promised to give His people, Pastors after His own heart, who will teach them knowledge and understanding if they return unto Him. Apostle John wrote to the Church concerning those who were seducing them through their own teachings (the teachings of man).(1 John 2:26)

The Lord Jesus Christ told His followers that they would receive the Spirit of truth, which the world cannot receive. This *Spirit of truth* (the Holy Spirit) is what the Apostle describes as the anointing that teaches you *"the chosen ones of God"* all things, because the Spirit has given gifts to men in the Church, who shall work in the vineyard of God to teach the people of God the truth about God's Word. (John 16:13)

No matter how anointed you may be, you still need a teacher to teach you what you do not know. God set up baptism as part of His plan to save His people from the very beginning. In Egypt, where the children of God were in bondage, the blood of lambs was shed for their deliverance but, on their way to the Promised Land, they were baptised in the cloud and in the Sea, under the leadership of Moses.

Moreover, brethren, I would not that ye should be ignorant, how that all our fathers were under the cloud, and all passed through the Sea. And were all baptised unto Moses in the cloud and in the Sea. And did all eat the same spiritual meat. And did all drink the same spiritual drink for they drank of that spiritual Rock that followed them, and that Rock was Christ (1 Corinthians 10:1-2)

Apostle Paul, during his days in ministry, told the Church in=] Corinth that they should not be ignorant of how their fathers were under the cloud, and all passed through the Sea and were baptised unto Moses. In these last days, the devil wants to change the writings of Apostle Paul to make him responsible for the fall of many people, but God by His divine revelation, has given His church the awareness by warning us through the same man of God. In his letter to the Romans, Paul tells them they are without excuse. If they allow the devil to divert them from the truth that the Apostles taught the Church. (see Romans 1:1-17) Do not blame him, because everything the Church needs to know has been written down right from the Garden of Eden.

The Steps to Genuine Salvation

The fall of man started from the sin of disobedient. After the sin, man was entangled in bondage. Sin gave man over to the curse and the curse gave man to death. Man was covered in darkness and began to walk in darkness, and started receiving direction from the god of darkness. This made the imaginations of man's heart evil. Before any man can get total salvation, he needs someone to pay the price by delivering him from sin through obedience.

Man needed someone to break the curse, which God pronounce on him after sin and not the ground. Man is still walking and toiling on this cursed earth, according to the pronouncement of God's Word upon him after his disobedience. God loves man and has given him an opportunity to be saved through Jesus Christ, our Saviour. The worldly *Man,* without Jesus, is dead; heading to destruction. Jesus came to deliver us from sin, curse and eternal death by giving us eternal life. Jesus took these three steps to save fallen man from sin, curse and death. Since it was disobedience that led *Adam* (mankind) away from God, Jesus Christ, the second Adam, became obedient unto death on the cross. He was rthen raised from the dead as the first fruit in leading man back to God. The Bible calls Him the first-born Son. The blood of Jesus Christ was shed to deliver our souls from the devil's prison of sin.

The body of Jesus Christ was nailed to the cross to deliver us from the curse that God pronounced upon man. He rose from the dead to deliver man from the bondage of eternal death by giving man's spirit *eternal life* so we could worship Him in truth and in spirit.

These are the genuine steps to man's salvation and, since the Lord Jesus came purposely to save man from these three areas of bondage, the true servants of God are given the message of salvation to preach and teach for the total freedom of the sons and daughters of Adam.

What Christianity is all about, is becoming a son or daughter of the second Adam who is the Lord God from heaven. It takes a New Birth to be born into the kingdom of God as a spiritual son or daughter. Any man who has never passed through the *born again* procedure, no matter how long he may have been in the Church or how highly he is positioned with titles and honours, will remain only as an image of God and not a child of God. Such a person will forever remain a cast away because Jesus Christ, our Lord and Saviour, is coming for the sons and daughters of the Kingdom. This makes the *born again* teachings and preaching the number one priority in the Kingdom's message of salvation.

Anybody born into this world has a father. So it is in the Kingdom's birth, which is spiritual. The second Adam, *the Lord from heaven,* is the father of His *born again* children. For this reason, the *born again* message is very important to Christians without which, no one can see or enter into the kingdom of God. It takes being born of water and of the Spirit to be transformed from an image of God *"the son of Adam"* to the son of *the second Adam* who came in the form of man, to give birth to the sons and daughters of man. This is why Jesus said the true worshipers shall worship the Lord in truth and in spirit.

CHAPTER FOUR

The Seal of Ownership

Unto Adam also and to his wife did the Lord God make coats of skins, and clothed them. (Genesis 3:21)

After the sin of Adam and Eve in the Garden of Eden, they discovered they were naked and covered themselves with leaves. Because the mercy of God was still upon them, He made a coat of animal skins and covered them. This tells us that blood was shed for their covering.

It was points to Jesus Christ, the Lamb of God, who would die on the cross, and shed His blood for the salvation of those who believe in Him. The Bible says those who are baptised into Christ have put on Christ, and that we shall be like Him when He shall appear.

Beloved, now are we the sons of God, and it doth not yet appear what we shall be; but we know that , when he shall appear, we shall be like him, for we shall see him as he is. (1John 3:2)

For ye are all the children of God by faith in Christ Jesus. For as many of you as have been baptised into Christ have put on Christ. There is neither Jew nor Greek, there is neither bond nor free, there is neither male nor female; for ye are all one in Christ Jesus. And if ye be Christ's, then are ye Abraham's seed and heirs according to the promise. (Galatians 3:26-29)

Combining the above scriptures, written by two apostles of Jesus Christ, Apostle John and Apostle Paul, we see they say the same thing, because they have the same Spirit of God. Apostle Paul has already written to the Galatian Church that, *as many that have been baptised into Christ have put on Christ*, while Apostle John also wrote to the Church that *we shall be like Him when He shall appear.*

It takes those who have *put on Christ* to be like Him when He appears for His saints during the rapture. The Apostolic doctrine does not contradict itself, so anything that the Apostles did not preach or teach, but is been preached and taught today in the Church, must be meticulously checked against the Scriptures to avoid the devil's deception. The devil is most certainly in the Church with his false doctrines.

Our Lord and Saviour, Jesus Christ, and His disciples warned the Church to be very careful about the doctrines of these last days. When division started in the Church in Corinth, Apostle Paul dealt with it and killed that spirit, knowing that division in the Church is the beginning of politics where people use their own minds to deceive their followers The people of God then become followers of men and not of God.

Now I beseech you. Brethren, by the name of our Lord Jesus Christ, that ye all speak the same thing, and that there be no divisions among you; but that ye be perfectly joined together in the same mind and in the same judgment. (1 Corinthians 1:10)

For I am jealous over you with godly jealousy. For I have espoused you to one husband that I may present you as a chaste virgin to Christ. But I fear lest by any means, as the serpent beguiled Eve through his subtlety, so your minds should be corrupted from the simplicity that is in Christ. For if he that cometh preached another Jesus, whom we have not preached, or if ye receive another Spirit, which ye have not received, or another gospel, which ye have not accepted, ye might well bear with him.
[13]For such are false apostles, deceitful workers, transforming themselves into the apostles of Christ. [14]And no marvel, for Satan himself is transformed into an angel of light. [15]Therefor it is no great thing if his ministers also be transformed as the ministers of righteousness, whose end shall be according to their works. (2 Corinthians 11:2-4, 13-15)

Apostle Paul did not keep silent despite the challenges he faced in his ministry from the false brethren (the ministers of Satan). They tried to stop him from the truth, which the Lord Jesus Christ had revealed to him on his way to Damascus while Paul was still persecuting the followers of Jesus Christ. There is no deception in the Church today that God has not revealed through His chosen servants whom He called of old, and is still calling, to proclaim the truth and to warn His people against the activities of false teachers and prophets.

In the Apostle's warning to the Church in Corinth concerning those who will deceive them with the Word of God, Paul quotes from Genesis where Satan deceived Eve through his subtlety. Satan turned her mind from the true *Word* of God to his own framed word that leads to death. In the the New Testament Church, the devil did the same thing, but could not succeed because the disciples of Jesus Christ were one, and were known by their doctrine. No other doctrine could be established during their days of ministration.

You may ask why we now have unresolved issues regarding the Word of God in the Church today when we claim to preach what the Apostles preached. They were able to resolve the issues that arose within the church of God during their time. The answer is simply that people, claiming to have received revelation of the Word of God, fail to teach the mind of God to His children like the Apostles did. They no longer fear God, so they interpret His Word to suit their purposes. Soul winning is no more their main goal, but merchandising of the Word of God.

We need to know that our God is not the author of confusion. Everything the Church needs to know is clearly stated in the Scriptures and we are instructed to study the Scriptures for proper understanding. Jesus taught His followers every teaching we hear today in the church of God. So we are without excuse.

Please read Matthew 13 for the parable the Lord told and explained to His disciples concerning the kingdom of God. Every false doctrine we hear and see in the Church today was established after the death of the Apostles.

Jesus said in His parable to His church, that *while men slept, the enemy came in and sowed tares among the wheat and went his way (Matthew 13:24-30)*. Apostle Paul, by revelation said, the saints that were dead had *fallen asleep.* This gives us the understanding that after the death of the disciples, the enemy established his doctrine in the Church. This doctrine is now mistakenly accepted as the truth in many Churches today. The Apostle did not leave us in darkness in these areas, so it is left to us to check our position in the Lord; if we are still in Him.

Read Apostle Paul's warning to the Church in the following Scriptures and be aware.

Wherefore I take you to record his day that I am pure from the blood of all men. For I have not shunned to declare unto you all the counsel of God. Take heed therefore unto yourselves, and to all the flock, over the which the Holy Ghost have made you overseers, to feed the church of God, which he hath purchased with his own blood.
For I know this, that after my departing shall grievous wolves enter in among you, not sparing the flock. Also of your own selves shall men arise, speaking perverse things, to draw away disciples after them? Therefore watch, and remember, that by the space of three years I ceased not to warn every one night and day with tears. (Acts 20:26-31)

And daily in the temple and in every house, they ceased not to teach and preach Jesus Christ. (Acts 5:42)

That they should seek the Lord, if haply they might feel after him, and find him, though he be not far from everyone of us. For in him we live, and move, and have our being; as certain also of your own poets have said, for we are also his offspring. (Acts 17:27-28)

We preach, teach and sing that in Him, we live, move and have our being. Our own words testify against us that there is an entrance into Him. If so, then we need to check from His Word, through which entrance we entered into Him, because the devil also seeks to destroy souls through the Word of God.

The Lord Jesus Christ did not cease from urging His disciples to warn their converts, who would be disciples after them, about the deceptions of the devil and his ministers. These ministers of Satan have now infiltrated the Church with their doctrine of deception; doing exactly what their father, the devil, did in the Garden of Eden: twisting the Word of God.

The foundation on which God placed man in the Garden of Eden is the Word of God. Following the devil's deception, man fell from God's Word. The Word became flesh in the midst of His people who are flesh and blood, to save them through the same Word; giving birth to them into His kingdom. As the sons of Adam, we are all dead without Jesus Christ. Before we can receive life, we need to enter into Jesus Christ who gives life through the New Birth.

That which was from the beginning, which we have heard, which we have seen with our eyes, which we have looked upon, and our hands have handled, of the word of life. (for the life was manifested, and we have seen it, and bear witness, and show unto you that eternal life, which was with the Father, and was manifested unto us). That which we have seen and heard declare we unto you, that ye also may have fellowship with us, and truly our fellowship is with the Father and with his Son Jesus Christ. (1 John 1:1-3)

We can have fellowship with the Father and His Son, Jesus Christ, but it must be through His disciples, because they were chosen by our Lord and Saviour, Jesus Christ, to continue the work that He started; that is His Church. They were called out to call others with the same voice that called them. Jesus said *my sheep heareth my voice, and a stranger will they not follow.* (John 10:27)

We cannot say we are Christians like the disciples of Jesus Christ, first called Christians in Antioch, if we preach another gospel other than the one given to the apostles by Jesus Christ. The gate that leads to the kingdom of God, that the Apostles of Jesus Christ preached to their converts, is doing everything in Jesus' name and not in the titles of *Father, Son,* and *Holy Spirit,* as recorded in Matthew.

CHAPTER FIVE

The Foundational Truth

He saith unto them, but whom say ye that I am? And Simon Peter answered and said, thou art the Christ, the Son of the living God. And Jesus answered and said unto him, blessed art thou, Simon Bar-Jona; for flesh and blood hath not revealed it unto thee, but my Father which is in heaven. And I say also unto thee, that thou art Peter, and upon this rock I will build my church, and the gates of hell shall not prevail against it. (Matthew 16:15-18)

Out of ignorance, we have been teaching many people that Peter was the rock on which the church of Jesus Christ is built. This is erroneous, because Peter himself confessed to the disciples that, out of his mouth came the word of salvation, which is Jesus Christ.

And when there had been much disputing. Peter rose up, and said unto them, men and brethren, ye know how that a good while ago God made choice among us, that the Gentiles by my mouth should hear the word of the gospel, and believe. (Acts 15:7)

Peter made it clear, that God has chosen him to speak the word of salvation unto people. The revelation that Peter had for our salvation is of Christ, the *Rock* on which Moses was placed in Exodus 33 for safety when the Lord passed by and allowed him to see His back. It is the same *Rock* which was in their midst as a man (the Son of God). Being in the form of man, His identity could only be discerned through revelation, which Peter received. It takes the Holy Spirit to reveal this to man who is of flesh and blood as it is the Spirit that searches the deep things of God.

The Bible teaches clearly that God has given us salvation through His only begotten son, Jesus Christ. It continues to say that *God has given us life, and the life is in the Son, and he who has the Son has life, he who has not the Son has not life.* (1 John 5:11)

This is where the problem lies, the entrance into *Son-ship* is the way to the Father. Jesus said, no *one goes to the Father but by me.* (John 14:6) Before Apostle Paul told Timothy that *great is the mystery of Godliness, that God was manifested in the flesh* (1 Timothy 3:16), he had already preached in Damascus that Christ is the son of God. Salvation makes Jesus Christ the son of God, but revelation makes Him the one true God who came in the flesh to save fallen man. This, the disciples baptised in Jesus' name as the foundation of the true Church. The one who died on the cross instead of man, is Jesus Christ, the son of God, He is the Father and the Holy Spirit.

A deeper revelation about our salvation will give us the understanding that the Father, Son and Holy Ghost are, together, the one true God of the Jews, come in the form of a man to reconcile man back unto Himself. The Father became a son to save His sons. He is the Holy Spirit that gives life to His children and dwells in them, and He is the true God whom His children call Father. This is the doctrine that the devil does not want man to practice, that made him create the belief of God in three persons, that is, the blessed Trinity.

Thou believest that there is one God; thou doest well: the devils also believe, and tremble. (James 2:19)

When a preacher stands to preach the oneness of God and that there is but one God, the kingdom of Satan trembles. This is the truth the devil has covered for years, but glory be to God for revealing it in these last days. This is the message of the Kingdom that Jesus said *shall be preached unto the whole world and then the end shall come.* (Matthew 24:14)

The question stands the same in the Bible; have you received the Holy Spirit since you believed? Into what baptism were you baptised? If you have not been baptised in Jesus' name for the remission of your sins, then what else can wash your sins away?

The Father is a spirit. He has no blood to wash away your sins. Neither has the Holy Spirit. It is only the Son, Jesus Christ, who came as flesh and blood, and died for sinner's sin, shedding His blood on the cross. Salvation of the cross can only be obtained through Jesus Christ, the son of God.

And this is the record that God hath given us eternal life, and this life is in the

Son. He that hath the Son hath life, and he that hath not the Son of God hath not life. (1John 5:11-12)

Repent and be baptised in Jesus' name for the remission of your sin. (Acts 2:28) One may say, I have been baptised in the name of the Father, the Son, and the Holy Ghost, so I do not need any baptism in water. I have the Holy Ghost with the evidence of speaking in tongues, so what else? You are a *Nicodemus* who must be born again.

Those who received the Holy Spirit from the beginning, baptised their converts in Jesus' name for the remission of their sins. If you are without sin, then you can be baptised in any name, but if you are a seed of Adam, then you are a sinner by birth (nature), and you need your sin to be washed away in the blood of Jesus through baptism in His name. That is why Nicodemus needed to be born again of water and of the Spirit, all in Jesus' name.

He was in the world, and the world was made by him, and the world knew him not, He came unto his own and his own received him not. But as many as received him to them gave him power to become the sons of God, even to them that believe on his name. Which were born, not of blood, nor of the will of the flesh, nor of the will of man, but of God. (John 1:10-14)

If we do not grasp the revelation of what happened on the cross where Jesus Christ died for man's sin, we will keep on arguing blindly over what we do not understand. On Calvary's cross, Jesus became like a sinner; He died for our sins and nailed our curse to the cross. This was why the Father, the Holy Ghost, separated Himself from Jesus.

After His death on the cross, He was brought down and placed in the tomb. Because the curse that was placed upon Him remained nailed to the cross, in the grave He became the Christ, *that Holy one.* The Holy Spirit entered into Him and resurrected Him again. Every human being can be saved through the cross if he can believe the gospel message about Jesus who died for sinners to be saved.

Repent and be baptised in Jesus' name for the remission of your sins and you shall receive the gift of the Holy Ghost.

The gate of Heaven is still open, so do not harden your heart.

Amen!

The Fall from the Foundational Truth

Many have fallen from the *foundational truth* by heeding to the devil's deception, just like Adam and Eve in the Garden of Eden. The Bible is full of examples to follow, which is why we are without excuse. God's Word can willingly be obeyed or disobeyed. Both have their rewards or consequences. We must all, as Christians, understand that, in the Church today, Satan has his ministers who preach and teach the Word of God just like God's chosen ministers, but with the motive of diverting the elect from the foundation of the truth.

Satan is called the *Old Serpent* in the Bible. (Revelation 12:9) This tells us that he is still in his old business of deceiving the people of God and this time not in the Garden of Eden but within the Church of God. When Satan got into the Garden of Gethsemane he quoted, *"it is written"* and Jesus (the word that became flesh) overcame him with, *"it is written".*

The main battle in the church of God today is the battle of doctrine. That is why Apostle Paul told his son, Timothy, to take heed unto himself and unto the doctrine, and by so doing he would save himself and those who would follow him. (1 Timothy 4:16) The Old Serpent *(Satan)* quoted the Word of God and twisted it in the Garden of Eden causing the people of God to fall from the foundational truth.

In the Garden of Gethsemane, the devil quotes from *Psalm 91* with the motive of destroying Jesus Christ's mission. Jesus also quotes from the Scripture, which showed His Lordship over Satan. This is an example for the followers of Jesus Christ. If Satan can do that to Jesus, then what do we think he is doing in the Church today with God's Word? In short, if Satan is diverting people from the truth, it must come from God's Word.

Let us read from the Scriptures what Apostle Peter recorded concerning Apostle Paul whom the Lord chose for the Gentiles.

Wherefore, beloved, seeing that ye look for such things, be diligent that ye may be found of him in peace, without spot, and blameless. And account that the long suffering of our Lord is salvation; even as our beloved brother Paul also according to the wisdom given unto him hath written unto you As also in all his epistles, speaking in them of these things, in which are some

things hard to be understood which they that are unlearned and unstable wrest, as they do also the other scriptures, unto their own destruction.
Ye therefore, beloved, seeing ye know these things before, beware lest ye also, being led away with the error of the wicked, fall from your own steadfastness. But grow in grace, and in the knowledge of our Lord and Saviour Jesus Christ. To him be glory both now and forever, Amen. (2 Peter 3:14-18)

Apostle Peter is writing to draw the attention of the Church to Apostle Paul's way of writing and the wisdom that God gave to him for the writing of the Scriptures. He made it plain that, according to the wisdom that God gave him, his writings are hard to understand without a teacher. Those who are unstable and unlearned, wrestle with Paul's Scripture as they do with other Scriptures, to their own destruction.

That means they often misquote Paul's words to their own destruction and the destruction of their followers They preach only how they understand the Word, and not what it really means. In the Garden of Eden, God spoke to Adam, who is the head, first, before the devil came in to speak to the woman; changing God's Word to fulfill his own purpose against humanity, which is *the fall of man from the foundation on which God placed him.* The devil is still busy with his business of deception.

It is our duty as Christians to search the Scriptures and trace the root of the *Apostolic foundation* and compare our faith to that of the Apostles; if we are fallen away or on the true foundation.

CHAPTER SIX

The Promise of New Birth

How then can man be justified with God? Or how can he be clean that is born of a woman? Behold even to the moon, and it shineth not; yea, the stars are not pure in his sight. How much less man, that is a worm? And the son of man, which is a worm? (Job 25:4-6)

There is therefore now no condemnation to them which are in Christ Jesus, who walk not after the flesh, but after the Spirit. For the law of the Spirit of life in Christ Jesus hath made me free from the law of sin and death. For what the law could not do, in that it was weak through the flesh, God sending his own Son in the likeness of sinful flesh, and for sin: That the righteousness of the law might be fulfilled in us, who walk not after the flesh, but after the Spirit. (Romans 8:1-4)

The church of Jesus Christ has diverted completely from the *Apostolic mission* into *prophetic deception* as I call it. The Church, which the Lord purchased with His own blood, is no longer teaching salvation that talks about New Birth, but rather of blessings, miracles, healing and so forth. We seem to have forgotten that the Bible says we should seek first the kingdom of God and all its righteousness and the rest shall be added unto us. (Matthew 6:33) The Church today lays so much more emphasis on worldly things *(physical things)* than the heavenly things.

Do not be deceived, our Lord and Saviour, Jesus Christ, is not coming for any denomination or people who have testimonies of one thing or the other, but for His children, who are born of water *(baptism)* and of the Spirit in His name. Life without Jesus and the New Birth will forever leave you the *son of Adam* and the image of God rather than the *son of God*.

Therefore, for man who is a descendant of Adam, to become a son of Jesus Christ *(The second Adam)*, on this earth, he must pass through the same process Jesus did. Repentance through obedience is to die and be buried with Him through baptism in His name. Resurrection in Him is through the baptism of the Holy Ghost in His name, with the evidence of speaking in tongues, as the Spirit gives the utterance.

We need to carry the cross daily on which the flesh is crucified in holiness. Apostle Paul declared that, *"I die daily."* (1 Corinthians 15:31) Our fleshly desires need to be nailed continuously to the cross. If you have not done these things, you are still only an image of God, and not the son of God.

It does not matter how long you have been in the Church, the number of miracles you perform, how richly and blessed you are, or your title in the Church; if you do not pass through these procedures, you are still an *image* of God, having the *Adam*-nature. The mystery behind the New Birth is spiritual, but can be explained in the physical through the understanding given to the Church by our Lord and Saviour, Jesus Christ. The Bible says: *The spirit of man is the candle of the Lord, searching all the inward parts of the belly.* (Proverbs 20:27.)

The New Birth experience is the tongue of fire *(The Holy Spirit)* from Heaven coming in contact with the tongue of flesh *(The spirit of man)* to enable him speak the heavenly language as proof of the resurrection of the dead spirit of man. The Apostle Paul explains the difference between praying with the spirit *(The tongue of fire)* and praying with understanding *(the tongue of flesh)* to the confused Corinthian church. The devil has succeeded in many Churches by telling the congregation that one can receive the Holy Ghost without speaking in tongues, this is a deceit.

Likewise the Spirit also helpeth our infirmities: for we know not what we should pray for as we ought: but the Spirit itself maketh intercession for us with groaning which cannot be uttered. And he that searcheth the hearts knoweth what is the mind of the Spirit, because he maketh intercession for the saints according to the will of God. (Romans 8:26)

Dead In Christ

This is repentance from sin. You have to accept Jesus Christ into your life, confess your sin and ask Him to come into your life and live a sin free life.

Buried with Christ

This is baptism in water in Jesus' name for the remission of your sins. Once you repent of your sins, you must be baptised in water in the name of Jesus Christ for the remission of your sins. Through this you are buried with Him in baptism.

Resurrected with Christ

This represents the Holy Spirit baptism with the evidence of speaking in tongues as the Spirit gives utterances. It is the Holy-Ghost-filled life known as the New Life in Christ, for the born again sons and daughters of Jesus Christ who live holy Christian lives. This is the only way that, a son of Adam can be transformed from the *image of God* to a son of God while on earth. Man is not created into the kingdom of God as Adam and his descendants were, but we are born again into the kingdom of God as the sons and daughters of Jesus Christ, the Lord from heaven, whom Apostle Paul referred to as the *second* Adam. (1 Corinthians 15:47}

Godliness

Christ like life with contentment is a great gain. (1 Timothy 6:6) The mystery of Godliness is God manifested in the flesh to give birth (born again) to flesh and blood with the heavenly nature while we are in this cursed world. Since this world is cursed, God has provided a world of blessings within Himself. That is why Jesus said: *In me you will have peace but in the world you will have tribulations.* (John 16:33) He used His servant Apostle Paul to confirmed by saying, *if any man be in Christ he is a new creature.* (2 Corinthians 5:17)

Disobedience

This brought sin, and sin brought curse, and curse brought death. So for Jesus to enter into the prison and bring His people out, He must pay the price for our sins through the shedding of His blood. He was nailed to the cross to pay for the curse pronounced upon man after sin, and was resurrected from death to pay the price of our dead spirit with His Spirit, by giving us the Holy Spirit.

There is therefore now no condemnation to them which are in Christ Jesus, who walk not after the flesh, but after the Spirit... (Romans 8:1)

But ye are not in the flesh, but in the Spirit. If so be that the Spirit of God dwell in you. Now if any man has not the Spirit of Christ, he is none of his. And if Christ be in you, the body is dead because of sin, but the Spirit is life because of righteousness. But if the Spirit of him that raised up Jesus from the dead dwell in you, he that raised up Christ from the dead shall also quicken your mortal bodies by his Spirit that dwelleth in you. (Romans 8:1, 9-11)

Apostle Paul, by revelation said the word that became flesh is the Lord from heaven, whom he referred to as the *second Adam.* (1 Corinthians 15:47) The first Adam, according to the Bible, is the father and the foundation of the human race. From Paul we understand that the second Adam, who is the Lord from heaven, came to give birth to sons and daughters of the first Adam who fell through sin, and transform them into His spiritual kingdom, which is the Church of Jesus Christ.

When God breathed into the first Adam, he became a living soul, but the process of the New Birth makes man a living spirit whose righteousness is of the Lord Jesus Christ. This is why the born again process must be the foundation of our teaching in the Church of Jesus Christ before other things, so that the children of God do not miss the real message of Christ's death.

The true servants of God must preach repentance from sins to fallen man. This is the primary assignment of a teacher of the Word. Every true child of God must know that Jesus Christ is the father of the Christians, and He dwells in them as the Holy Spirit. The evidence of this is seen in 1 John 4:4, which says, *greater is He who is in us (the Christians) than he who is in the world.* This makes Him the Lion that dwells in His sheep.

The New Birth is the greatest gift God has ever given to man and that is what makes the angels envious of man. God created everything, including Adam and Eve, yet by His divine mercy He has given us, *the sons of Adam,* this great opportunity to be born again into His kingdom in the name of Jesus Christ. Therefore, there is no excuse if we neglect this salvation, which is being taught and preached throughout the whole world by His chosen servants.

The mystery behind the *resurrection power* is the tongue of fire from the Holy Spirit, which is poured into man's spirit from Heaven to give life and light to the spirit of man that died and was cast out after the sin of disobedience. After sin, darkness fell on the spirit of man, separating him from his maker, leaving him to walk in total darkness. Every effort to return to God has been in vain if not for His grace.

The building of the *Tower of Babel* is an example of man's own creative way of seeking God. (see Genesis 11) In the New Birth, God is not breathing into the nostrils of man as He did to Adam, but is pouring His spirit into the spirit of man; giving life spiritually. Every living being makes noise as proof of the receipt of the breath of life. Likewise, for the Holy Spirit of Christ, there is always the evidence of speaking with the Heavenly language *(speaking in tongues)* as the Spirit gives the utterance. This is done to fulfill the prophecy of Prophet Joel. (Joel 2:28)

The spirit of God is what gives birth to the spirit of man by transforming the son of Adam who is a living soul into a living spirit.

So then they that are in the flesh cannot please God. But ye are not in the flesh, but in the Spirit, if so be that the Spirit of God dwell in you. Now if any man has not the Spirit of Christ he is none of his. – For as many as are led by the Spirit of God, they are the sons of God. (Romans 8:8-10, 14)

This is the main Apostolic doctrine. Our efforts and good works without the New Birth, are useless in the sight of God, because they make the birth, the suffering, and the death of Jesus Christ, on the cross, fruitless or meaningless. Man will always remain an *image of God* unless he passes through the process of the New Birth, of water and of the Spirit in Jesus' name. That is, putting on the name of Jesus Christ (Righteousness) by water baptism, and receiving the Holy Spirit baptism, which is *Christ in me the hope of glory.*

Jesus showed His disciples the example of *son-ship*, by telling them, *"I am in the Father and the Father is in me"*. (John 10:38) If man, an image of God, receives the gospel with total repentance and is baptised in Jesus' name for the remission of his sins, he enters into the Father. If he receives the Holy Ghost baptism, the Father comes in to dwell in him, and he becomes like Jesus Christ. Moreover, the Bible says we shall be like Him when He appears. Through water baptism, our sins are washed away, and we put the garment of righteousness on our soul through the name of Jesus, the only name given nto fallen man for salvation.

But we are all as an unclean thing, and all our righteousness are as filthy rags; and we all do fade as a leaf; and our iniquities, like the wind, have taken us away. (Isaiah 64:6)

While Peter yet spake these words, the Holy Ghost fell on all them which heard the word. And they of the circumcision which believed were astonished, as many as came with Peter, because that on the Gentiles also was poured out the gift of the Holy Ghost. For they heard them speak with tongues, and magnify God. Then answered Peter, Can any man forbid water, that these should not be baptised, which have received the Holy Ghost as well as we? And he commanded them to be baptised in the name of the Lord. Then prayed they him to tarry certain days. (Acts 10:44-48)

CHAPTER SEVEN

Assurance of the New Birth

The question behind the universal claims of *I am born again* is this: are you born again out of the promise of God(righteousness), or from the suggestion of man (flesh)?

To be sure of our salvation, we must know, from the Scriptures, that we are born again according to the promise of God not by the suggestion of man. It is very dangerous to walk with God with your own suggestion. To be saved and have peace with the Lord, you need to walk in obedience unto His commandments and you will receive His promises. Anything outside the promises of God will give birth to very big problems, which may lead you into bondage. If care is not taken, this may end you in the Lake of Fire. The Bible says *obedience is better than sacrifice.* (1 Samuel 15:22)

When God gave Abraham the promise of a son, He swore by Himself (Righteousness) to prove that no matter how it may delay, He would cause it to come to pass to fulfill His faithfulness unto him. During the cause of waiting, Sarah, Abraham's wife, suggested he take Hagar, her handmaid, as a wife in a way of helping the promise of God to be fulfilled. So Abraham, the father of faith, yielded to the advice of his wife and through Hagar, he had a son whom he named Ishmael. This is now the source of most of the problems in the world today. Because he was born out of carnality (the suggestion of man), the Lord ordered Abraham to cast him out from his house (Genesis16:10-16)

According to the Scripture, the child that would be born in Abraham's house by Hagar shall be a wild man whose hand shall be against every man, and every man's hand shall be against him. Since he was born out of a man's suggestion, he was cast out from the house of Abraham according to God's commandment to Abraham and became the number one enemy of the promised son of Abraham, Isaac, whose descendants are the Jews. This is why no man can stop the conflict between the Israelites, the Palestinians and their Arab brothers who are the descendants of Ishmael.

Everything that is going on in this world has its own foundation on which it operates. The religious conflicts in this evil world will not stop until the *New World,* which the Lord has promised, is established. (Revelation 21:1) Abraham, the father of many nations, according to God's promise to him when he had no son or daughter, had his first son out of the suggestion that came from Sarah, his wife. Hagar became the mother of the son born out of this suggestion. We should not forget that it was a suggestion that the devil gave to the woman (Eve) about the forbidden fruit that caused the fall of man from the Garden of Eden.

To understand what is going on in this religious world where fallen man is looking for his Creator through every means, we should not forget that the enmity between the Jews (descendants of Isaac) and the Arabs (descendants of Ishmael) shall never cease untilll the end of this evil era.

It is the same with other religions born out of somebody's suggestion and not from the *promise* of God, who is Jesus Christ, the son of the living and the one true God; crucified for our redemption through His blood. Every religion that is born out of man's suggestion, and not by the spirit of God through His spoken Word (Jesus Christ) will continue to persecute the promised children of God who are born out of His promise (Jesus Christ) through the Holy Spirit.

For it is written, that Abraham had two sons, the one by a bondmaid, the other by a freewoman. But he who was of the bondwoman was born after the flesh, but he of the freewoman was by promise. Which things are allegories, for these are the two covenants, the one from the Mount Sinai, which gendereth to bondage, which is Agar. For this Agar is Mount Sinai in Arabia, and answereth to Jerusalem which now is, and is in bondage with her children. But Jerusalem which is above is free, which is the mother of us all.
For it is written, rejoice, thou barren that bearest not, break forth and cry, thou that travailest not, for the desolate hath many more children than she which hath a husband. Now we brethren, as Isaac was, are the children of

promise. But as then he that was born after the flesh persecuted him that was born after the Spirit, even so it is now. Nevertheless what saith the scriptures? Cast out the bondwoman and her son for the son of the bondwoman shall not be heir with the son of the free woman. So then, brethren, we are not children of the bondwoman, but of the free. (Galatians 4:22-31)

The global religious battle that is going on shall not cease until the Church is taken to glory. Although Ishmael was born out of the suggestion of Sarah, Abraham's wife, God promised to bless him and make him a great nation because he was a son of Abraham. If we consider these two sons of Abraham, and compare them to the born-again children of God, the spiritual sons and daughters of Abraham, we then know where we belong. Everything that God wants us to know is stated in His Word. So it is time for us to check the source of our New Birth and see if we are born again out of God's promise or out of a man's suggestion.

When Jesus Christ sent the seventy disciples out, they came back to Him rejoicing that demons are subject to them. Jesus told them not to be happy because demons are subjects to them but they rather that their names are written in the Book of Life. (Luke 10:20) The Lord Jesus Christ gave the New Birth promise to the world by giving us the pattern and the plan of how to be born again. Anything other than this is a man's suggestion, which will take you away from the kingdom of God just like Ishmael whom God made great, but was cast out.

There are many men and women of God who claim to be born again, and to have seen the Lord Jesus Christ, yet they keep on persecuting and pulling each other down. Do our own actions not indicate that there are Ishmaels (outcasts) and Isaacs (promised sons) in the house of Abraham? We all claim Christianity, which qualifies us as spiritual children of Abraham through Jesus Christ.

There are two groups of Christians in the house of God today. The first group are born again according to the Apostles' doctrine with Jesus Christ being their foundation and who do everything including baptism) in the name of Jesus Christ. The second group baptise in the name of the Father, the Son and the Holy Ghost. However, this second group, when it comes to casting out demons or praying for the sick, they use the name of Jesus Christ. Is this not the reason why our Lord and Saviour, Jesus Christ, gave us the parable of the two ways, the narrow and the broad way? (Matthew 7:13)

I once met a young man at Cividale, a town near Udine in Italy, who asked me during a Bible discussion what would happen if he preached to somebody and that person receive the Word of God but could not be baptised in water before he died. Did this mean the person would not be saved? I replied that the young man shall not see nor enter into the kingdom of God. The man was shocked at this answer and asked me about the thief on the cross that Jesus Christ had promised to take to Paradise. Did he get baptised? I told him that this is where many are going to hell for the lack of knowledge.

The Bible says *he who the Lord sends, speaks the Word of God* (John 3:34), and the Word of God *(Jesus Christ)* says that, unless a man is born of water and of the Spirit he cannot see nor enter into the kingdom of God. This is what the early disciples preached and taught the church of Jesus Christ who were looking for salvation.

We must understand that God's dealings with man in saving him from dispensation to dispensation, is not always the same. In Egypt, God used the blood of animal sacrifice to deliver His people from the hands of Pharaoh and the Egyptians. On their way to the promise land, the crossing of the Red Sea became a symbol of water baptism according to the scriptures. (Numbers 20:11)

During the time of Noah, the Lord saved Noah and few souls by water when He commanded Noah to build the Ark and enter into it.

Moreover, brethren, I would not that ye should be ignorant, how that all our fathers were under the cloud, and all passed through the sea; And were all baptised unto Moses in the cloud and in the sea; And did all eat the same spiritual meat; And did all drink the same spiritual drink: for they drank of that spiritual Rock that followed them. And that Rock was Christ. (1 Corinthians 10:1-4)

Which sometime were disobedient, when once the longsuffering of God waited in the days of Noah, while the ark was a-preparing, wherein few, that is, eight souls were saved by water. The like figure whereunto even baptism doth also now save us (not the putting away of the filth of the flesh, but the answer of a good conscience toward God,) by the resurrection of Jesus Christ. (1 Peter 3:20-21)

And he said unto them, Go ye into all the world, and preach the gospel to every creature. He that believeth and is baptised shall be saved; but he that believeth not shall be damned. And these signs shall follow them that believe; In my name shall they cast out devils; they shall speak with new tongues. (Mark 16:15-17)

In this present Church dispensation, God is saving man with water, blood and His spirit in a different yet perfect way

And there are three that bear witness in earth, the spirit, the Word, and the blood: and these three agree in one. (1 John 5:8)

Jesus said unless a man is born again (baptised with water) and born again (baptised of the Spirit), he cannot see or enter into the kingdom of God. It is this *New Birth* that makes man the son of the last Adam who is the Lord from heaven. The Bible states clearly that the sons of God (the angels) in heaven are created beings meaning they are spirit beings and do not have the spirit of God in them. Only the sons and daughters of men, born again with water and of the Spirit, into the kingdom of God, have His spirit within them. The angels may well be jealous of us.

This is the greatest opportunity God has given to man in saving him. You must not allow yourself to be deceived by any self-appointed preacher or teacher who does not understand the meaning and purpose of why a man must be born again. They are in the ministry to deceive people with their imaginations of God's Word into destruction in Hell's fire.

The thief on the cross was saved under the dispensation of the Law, but after the day of Pentecost, marking the establishment of the Church, if you are not born again with water and of the Spirit, as Jesus commanded, you cannot enter into the kingdom of God. This is the Word of our Lord and Saviour, Jesus Christ, to the people who want to enter into the kingdom of God.

The Bible says *God is not a man that He should lie, neither the son of man that He should repent, hath He said, and shall He not do it? or hath He spoken, and shall He not make it.* (Numbers 23:19)

When studying God's Word, we must be very careful we do not apply the Word of God wrongly to our own destruction. God promised to make Ishmael a great nation even though he was born out of the suggestion of Sarah since he, also, was a seed of Abraham. If we compare the way in which the the two sons of Abraham were born, it may help us to trace the foundation on which we are born again. This is either by the Word of God (Jesus Christ) or by somebody's suggestion of the Word of God such as the suggestion the devil gave to Eve in the Garden of Eden or to Jesus Christ when he tempted Him.

If we can compare the two sons that were born in the house of Abraham to the born again children of God in the house of God today, it will help us to come out from every bondage of deception brought on by the suggestion of man (the doctrine of man), which is not the *truth.* The early disciples of Jesus Christ did everything, including baptism, in *Jesus' name* and not in the titles of God the Father, God the Son and God the Holy Spirit. The mysteries of the kingdom was given to them by Jesus Christ Himself, according to Matthew 13:11. They preached repentance from sins and baptism in Jesus' name for the remission of sins and receiving the gift of the Holy Ghost with the evidence of speaking in tongues.

Then opened he their understanding, that they might understand the scriptures. And said unto them, thus it is written, and thus it behooved Christ to suffer, and to rise from the dead the third day. And that repentance and remission of sins should be preached in his name among all nations, beginning at Jerusalem. And ye are witnesses of these things. And behold, I send the promise of my Father upon you; but tarry ye in the city of Jerusalem, until ye be endued with power from on high. (Luke 24:45-49)

Let the word of Christ dwell in you richly in all wisdom; teaching and admonishing one another in psalms and hymns and spiritual songs, singing with grace in your hearts to the Lord. And whatsoever ye do in word or deed, do all in the name of the Lord Jesus, giving thanks to God and the Father by him. (Colossians 3:16-17)

There is one body, and one Spirit, even as ye are called in one hope of your calling. One Lord, one faith, one baptism. One God and Father of all who is above all, and through all, and in you all. (Ephesians 4:4-6)

A careful study of the above scriptures will help us ascertain, if you were born again by our Father and Lord Jesus Christ through the apostolic message preached on the day of Pentecost, or by somebody's suggestions out of the Word of God. The number one enemy of the children of God is those believers who claim they are born again, but not according to the promise of God through Jesus Christ, but from their own suggestions out of their own imaginations. Those who are born again out of people's suggestions take the position of the Pharisees in persecuting the children of God who knows their Father as Jesus Christ the *Lord God* from heaven who came to die for His children in saving them.

As Ishmael (the son born out of suggestion) persecuted Isaac (the son born out of God's promise), so are the true children of God, going to be persecuted by the people Apostle Paul called *false brethren* and *false apostles.* These are people who interpret the Word of God with their own imaginations and suggestions to their own destruction. They will never stop fighting against the true sons and daughters of Jesus Christ who are holding unto the *truth* until the rapture.

Now we, brethren, as Isaac was are the children of promise. But as then he that was born after the flesh persecuted him that was born after the Spirit, even so it is now. (Galatians 4:28-29)

This book wants to help you check the lineage of your spiritual. Are you are born again according to the apostolic doctrine, the doctrine of man, or the doctrine of the devil? The devil persuaded Eve to eat the forbidden fruit, out of his own suggestion, using the Word of God. It is time for you to free yourself from people's interpretations out of God's Word that lead to bondage and ultimately into the Lake of Fire.

CHAPTER EIGHT

The Difference between Christians and Believers.

Little children, it is the last time, and as ye have heard that antichrist shall come, even now are there many antichrists, whereby we know that it is the last time. They went out from us, but they were not of us, for if they had been of us, they would no doubt have continued with us, but they went out, that they might be made manifest that they were not all of us. (1John 2:18-19)

For many deceivers are entered into the world, who confess not that Jesus Christ is come in the flesh. This is a deceiver and an antichrist. Look to yourselves that we lose not those things which we have wrought, but that we receive a full reward. Whosoever transgresseth, and abideth not in the doctrine of Christ, hath not God. He that abideth in the doctrine of Christ, he hath both the Father and the Son. If there come any unto you and bring not this doctrine, receive him not into your house, neither bid him God speed. For he that biddeth him God speed is partaker of his evil deeds. (2 John 7-11)

Now therefore ye are no more strangers and foreigners, but fellow citizens with the saints, and of the household of God. And are build upon the foundation of the Apostles and Prophets, Jesus Christ himself being the chief corner stone. In whom all the building fitly framed together growth unto an Holy temple in the Lord. In whom ye also are builded together for an habitation of God through the Spirit. (Ephesians 2:19-22)

Any distraction from the Apostles' doctrine is not from the Lord Jesus Christ, no matter how nicely it is polished and presented as the truth to the children of God. It is a deception that leads to death. We need to compare whatever doctrine taught in the house of God to that of the Apostles.

Today some churches have introduced the worship of Mary, angels and saints (the dead) into their religion, calling it Christianity (church of Jesus

Christ). Their members are made to worship images of such people, which the Lord God, the Father Almighty, forbade since the days of Moses, His servant. These churches have introduced their religious abominations into the church of God; making it to seem right in the sight of the people of God who blindly accept it as truth.

Let no man therefore judge you in meat, or in drink, or in respect of an holyday, or of the new moon, or of the Sabbath days. Which are a shadow of things to come, but the body is of Christ. Let no man beguile you of your reward in a voluntary humility and worshipping of angels, intruding into those things which he hath not seen, vainly puffed up by his fleshly mind, and not holding the Head, from which all the body by joints and bands having nourishment ministered, and knit together, increaseth with the increase of God.
Wherefore if ye be dead with Christ from the world, why, as though living in the world, are ye subject to ordinances, (Touch not taste not, handle nor, which all are to perish with the using) after the commandments and doctrine of men? Which things have indeed a show of wisdom in will-worship, and humility, and neglecting of the body, not in any honour to the satisfying of the flesh. (Colossians 2:16-23)

The conflict between religious *sects* shall not stop until the end of the world since it is a spiritual battle. Every religion that is not the true Christianity, which is founded on Jesus Christ, is formed to fight against the true children of Jesus Christ who are the saints. Somebody may claim he has now come to the knowledge of the truth, by changing his religion. This may be true or not, because changing from one religion to another is nothing more than swimming in the devil's ocean of deception.

The persecution of Christians is not a new thing. If we trace the history of the Church, we can understand it better. Christians, from the time of the Apostles, were persecuted by religious sects and, since such religious institutions still exist, they will continue to persecute the saints until the rapture. This is why the Lord said if He did not cut short the days, no flesh can be saved.(Matthew 24:22) Many Christians today respond to the spirit of the antichrist's calling for believers to meet either for prayer or for religious discussion, without knowing that it is the spirit of deception.

The strategy the devil uses is to eliminate any doctrine from the Church so that they can lead the people of God to himself. This is one reason the Church no longer teaches or preaches the doctrine of Christ, which is the seal of the true church of Jesus Christ. It is also a main cause of their persecution. When Jesus Christ came to the earth, there were the Pharisees, the Sadducees and other religious groups, but it was the doctrine He taught the Apostles that separated them from these. This doctrine still separates the true church of Jesus Christ from the other religions. If the followers of Jesus Christ are not being persecuted today as He said, then we must know that we have diverted from the *narrow way* that teaches and preaches the doctrine of Christ.

Now about the midst of the feast Jesus went up into the temple, and taught. And the Jews marveled, saying, how knoweth this man letters, having never learned? Jesus answered them, and said, my doctrine is not mine, but his that sent me. If any man will do his will, he shall know of the doctrine, whether it be of God, or whether I speak of myself. (John 7:14-17)

Jesus Christ came as a Jew, from the lineage of David but what separated Him and His followers from His brethren, is the doctrine He brought and taught His disciples to teach their followers who were called Christians for the first time in Antioch. Jesus told His disciples to be careful of the doctrine of the Pharisees and of the Sadducees when He was in their midst. (Matthew 16:6) Now that He is dwelling in His saints as the Holy Spirit (Emmanuel), what will He be telling His church about the doctrines that are being taught in His church throughout the whole world?

During the days of His teachings, the Lord told His disciples to be careful of the doctrine of the Pharisees and of the Sadducees, who were Jews, God's chosen people. Today, the Lord is telling His Church to be careful of the doctrine of the people who call themselves Christians but have not embraced the doctrine of Christ. They are the people who persecuted the true disciples of Jesus Christ, and will continue persecute the true Church until the rapture.

The Apostle Paul was drawn out from a group of persecutors to become a preacher of the very doctrine for which they were persecuting the Apostles. Because he was called out from the persecutors of that same doctrine, he realised that it was by God's grace that he knew the truth. He told this to

Timothy, his son in the Lord.

According to the glorious gospel of the blessed God, which was committed to my trust. And I thank Christ Jesus our Lord, who hath enabled me, for that he counted me faithful, putting me into the ministry. Who was before a blasphemer, and a persecutor, and injurious: but I obtained mercy, because I did it ignorantly in unbelief. (1 Timothy 1:11-13)

 But the same group of persecutors turned against Paul, persecuting him from city to city and even requested that he should be killed for blaspheming against the doctrine of Moses, which is the doctrine of the Jews, and preaching and teaching that Jesus Christ, who was crucified, is the Lord God of the Jews.

Let us see from the Scriptures how Paul defends the doctrine of Christ given to him by revelation when he was arrested for preaching it.

And one Ananias, a devout man according to the law, having a good report of all the Jews which dwelt there. Came unto me, and stood, and said unto me, Brother Saul, receive thy sight. And the same hour I looked up upon him. And he said. The God of our fathers hath chosen thee, that thou shouldest know his will, and see that Just One, and shouldest hear the voice of his mouth.
For thou shalt be his witness unto all men of what thou hast seen and heard. And now why tarriest thou? Arise, and be baptised, and wash away thy sins, calling on the name of the Lord. And it came to pass, that, when I was come again to Jerusalem, even while I prayed in the temple, I was in a trance; And saw him saying unto me, Make haste, and get thee quickly out of Jerusalem: for they will not receive thy testimony concerning me.
And I said, Lord, they know that I imprisoned and beat in every synagogue them that believed on thee. And when the blood of thy martyr Stephen was shed, I also was standing by, and consenting unto his death, and kept the raiment of them that slew him. And he said unto me, depart for I will send thee far hence unto the Gentiles. And they gave him audience unto this word, and then lifted up their voices, and said, away with such a fellow from the earth, for it not fit that he should live. (Acts 22:12-22)

Today it is only God who knows how many persecutors of the Apostolic doctrine there are to whom the truth has been revealed, yet are afraid to preach it publicly. They have been in the persecuting group for such a long time and they know they would be persecuted themselves should they keep on preaching and teaching this doctrine Sadly, many men of God are living in compromise, knowing the truth, but rejecting it when it comes to defending the Apostolic doctrine.

The devil knows very well that if he succeeds in removing the doctrine of Jesus Christ from the Church, it will turn to another religion instead of Christianity. His demons are working very hard in removing any doctrine from the Church. This is why we hear men of God telling their congregations that they are not concerned with doctrine.

Many people are being deceived by the miracles, signs and wonders they see the so-called men of God perform as a sign of the true servant of God. Some do not know that the devil often heals, blesses and imitates the things of Jesus Christ, performing miracles, signs, wonders and so forth. I have heard of a man of God, invited by some pastors into a city, telling the people to forget about *doctrine* and come together to work for Jesus Christ. He explained how doctrine separates churches so if the Church did not do away with *doctrine,* they would not come together in anything.

To the lost and condemned Church, such a statement sounds good, but to the living church of Jesus Christ, it is discerned as the voice of the spirit of the antichrist whose coming is after Satan, as Apostle Paul explains to the Thessalonian Church. (2 Thessalonians 2)

I have personally heard a pastor tell a member of a church that *doctrine* does not save. I humbly reminded the man of God that, our Lord Jesus Christ is saving His people through the doctrine that He brought from heaven. Christ handed over to His disciples to preach to His church so as to save them. We are saved by the doctrine of Christ and not by every wind of doctrine.

Let us see from the Scriptures, Apostle Paul's position on this.

For therefore we both labour and suffer reproach, because we trust in the living God, who is the savior of all men, especially of those that believe. These things command and teach. Let no man despise thy youth; but be thou an example of the believers, in word, in conversation, in charity, in spirit, in faith, in purity.

Till I come, give attendance to reading, to exhortation, to doctrine. Neglect not the gift that is in thee, which was given thee by prophecy, with the laying on of the hands of the presbytery. Meditate upon these things; give thyself wholly to them; that thy profiting may appear to all. Take heed unto thyself and unto the doctrine; continue in them; for in doing this thou shall both save thyself, and them that hear thee. (1Timothy 4:10-16)

If we remove the *doctrine of Jesus Christ*, the seal of the true Church, from His church, it falls to another religion that has no power, to save a fallen man. This is what the spirit of the antichrist is. It is his mission to empty heaven into hell while the spirit of Jesus Christ's goal is to empty hell into heaven. Many people have asked questions like, what is the doctrine of Christ? How can I know if I am in the church of Jesus Christ or not? Unfortunately, their question is not answered according to the biblical truth who is Jesus Christ, so they end up being confused.

The writer of Hebrews explained just what the doctrine of Christ is all about:

Therefore leaving the principles of the doctrine of Christ, let us go on unto perfection; not laying again the foundation of repentance from dead works, and of faith toward God, Of the doctrine of baptisms, and of laying on of hands, and of resurrection of the dead, and of eternal judgment. (Hebrews 6:1-2)

CHAPTER NINE

The Pillar of the True Church of Jesus Christ

These things write I unto thee, hoping to come unto thee shortly: But if I tarry long, that thou mayest know how thou oughtest to behave thyself in the house of God, which is the church of the living God, the pillar and ground of the truth. And without controversy great is the mystery of godliness; God was manifest in the flesh, justified in the Spirit, seen of angels, preached unto the Gentiles, believed on in the world, received up into glory. (1 Timothy 3:14-16)

The foundation on which the Church of Jesus Christ was built is *Jesus Christ* Himself. It states in Revelation that Jesus Christ was crucified before the foundation of the earth.(Revelation 13:8) The Bible has the answer to every question, but the understanding is what the Church is lacking. Many self-appointed ministers of God have entered into the Church causing confusion with the way they interpret the things of God with their own imagination. Many of God's chosen servants who want to be like the other ministers, fall away from their God's given duty.

Many Christians today are followers of people and not of Jesus Christ. We always hear some Christians say, "my Pastor said this or that" and not, "Jesus Christ or His servant, Apostle Paul said this or that." The above Scripture will help you to understand the doctrine of Christ, which was prophesied after the fall (the sin) of man, for our salvation, which was hidden in Christ Jesus. The Bible says Jesus Christ is the same *yesterday, today and forever*. (Hebrews 3:18)

The Apostle Paul wrote to Timothy, his son in the Lord, to let him know how he should conduct himself in the house of God, which is the church of the living God, the Pillar and the ground of the *Truth.*

Paul goes on to say, *and without controversy great is the mystery of godliness, God was manifested in the flesh, justified in the Spirit, seen of angels, preached unto the Gentiles, believed on in the world, received up into glory.* (1 Timothy 3:16)

Apostle Paul, the preacher and teacher, that Jesus Christ Himself arrested on his way to Damascus to persecute the true church of God, has made the matter clear for us by the revelation the Lord Jesus Christ gave him. He states that the *pillar and the ground* on which the t*rue church of Jesus Christ* is built, is the revelation of the one true God, manifest in the flesh in the person of Jesus Christ.

This is what was revealed to Apostle Peter by the heavenly Father, who is a spirit, when Jesus asked His disciples, *whom do you also say that I, the Son of man, am? When others say I am Elijah or one of the Prophets.* Peter's respond is *thou art the Christ, the Son of the living God.* (Matthew 16:16) The Christ is the anointed body in which the Father, who is a spirit, dwelled to save His people, who are flesh and blood, whose dwelling place is on the earth.

The angel who appeared to Joseph during the conception of Jesus Christ by Mary, quoted from the book of Isaiah 7:14, *Therefore the Lord himself shall give you a sign; Behold, a virgin shall conceive, and bear a son, and shall call his name Emmanuel, which being interpreted, God with us.*

Because the Christ is who Mary birthed after the Holy Ghost over-shadowed her, Jesus called Himself the *son of man* and, at the same time, the *son of God*. The combination of the Holy Spirit and man (Mary). Revelation shows Jesus Christ as the *Lamb of God* and the *Lion of the tribe of Judah*. (Revelation 5:5) Apostle Paul said, God (the Father) was in Christ (the Son-flesh) reconciling the world unto Himself, and it is done through baptism. (2 Corinthians 5:19)

If you repent and are baptised in the name of Jesus Christ for the remission of your sins, you enter into Christ (Son-ship). If you receive the Holy Spirit with the evidence of speaking in tongues, the Father (Holy Spirit) will come and dwell in you. You will become like Jesus Christ who was a man and, at the same time, a spirit. You can then contact your Father who is in heaven through His spirit, which dwells in you. In the book of Hebrews, this doctrine of Christ is comprehensively explained to the Church.

Therefore leaving the principles of the doctrine of Christ, let us go on unto perfection; not laying again the foundation of repentance from dead works, and of faith toward God, of the doctrine of baptisms, and of laying on of hands, and of resurrection of the dead, and of eternal judgment. And this will we do, if God permit. (Hebrews 6:1-3)

The writer of Hebrews has explained the doctrine of Christ and has made it very simple for the Church. He goes on to say, *therefore leaving the principles of the doctrine of Christ, let us go on unto perfection.* In the following chapter (Hebrews 7), the author gives an explanation of Melchisedec who was the king of peace to whom Abraham paid tithe.

This was the Scripture that Jesus Christ referred to when he told the Jews that, *your father Abraham rejoiced to see my day: and he saw it, and was glad. The said the Jews unto Him, you are not yet fifty years old and you are saying you saw our father Abraham, and he still replied them saying, Verily, verily I say unto you, before Abraham was, I am.* (John 8:56-58)

That statement was blasphemy to the Jews because they knew that their father, Abraham, had seen God in a human form. When Jesus said, *your father Abraham saw me and was glad*, the Jews quickly understood that Jesus was claiming to be the one true God of the Jews whom their father Abraham had seen. They wanted to stone Him for blasphemy, because He, a man, was making Himself, God.

In Hebrews 7:1-4 the writer says, *For this Melchisedec, king of Salem, priest of the most high God, who met Abraham returning from the slaughter of the kings, and blessed him; To whom also Abraham gave a tenth part of all; first being by interpretation King of righteousness, and after that also King of Salem, which is, King of peace; Without Father, without mother, without descent, having neither beginning of days, nor end of life; but made like unto the Son of God; abideth a priest continually. Now consider how great this man was, unto whom even the patriarch Abraham gave the tenth of the spoils.*

Howbeit we speak wisdom among them that are perfect: yet not the wisdom of this world, nor of the princes of this world, that come to nought:

But we speak the wisdom of God in a mystery, even the hidden wisdom, which God ordained before the world unto our glory: Which none of the princes of this world knew: for had they known it, they would not have crucified the Lord of glory. (1 Corinthians 2:6-8)

The above Scripture gives us the needed understanding as to why our Lord and Saviour, Jesus Christ, came and died for us. Apostle Paul explains to us that the crucifixion of Jesus Christ, which was for the salvation of fallen man, was a hidden wisdom of God to destroy the works of Satan and his demons. Man can now freely come to his maker and worship Him through the gospel. Paul says that if the princes of this world had known that the blood of Jesus Christ would destroy their works and liberate their prisoners, they would not have crucified the Lord of glory according to the Scriptures.

The *pillar* on which the true church of God is built is the revelation of Jesus, the Christ; the manifestation of God in the flesh as the Lamb of God to die for His sheep in saving them from their sins. This is why Revelation refers to Jesus Christ as the Lamb of God and at same time the Lion of the tribe of Judah.

The foundation, on which the one true church of God is built, is conducting everything in Jesus' name, including baptism. When you come to the knowledge that Jesus Christ is the Lord, remember to be baptised in His name for the remission of your sins, as it is written: *All have sinned and have come short of the glory of God.* (Romans 3:23)

CHAPTER TEN

The True Identity

Then saith he to his servant, the wedding is ready, but they which were biden were not worthy. Go ye therefore into the highways, and as many as ye shall find, bid to the marriage. So those servants went out into the highways, and gathered together all as many as they found, both bad and good: and the wedding was furnished with guests.
And when the king came in to see the guests, he saw there a man which had not on a wedding garment: And he saith unto him, Friend, how camest thou in hither not having a wedding garment? And he was speechless. Then said the king to the servants, Bind him hand and foot, and take him away, and cast him into outer darkness; there shall be weeping and gnashing of teeth. For many are called, but few are chosen. (Matthew 22:8-14)

Understanding the parables of Jesus Christ is one of the greatest blessings the Lord has given to His disciples, rather than just the working of miracles, which many people lust after in these last days. Many people claim to receive messages directly from God but lack the spiritual knowledge of revealing God's heart to His church.

It is one thing to hear from God, and it is another thing to understand His words. In short, man is given the grace to search the Scriptures, and save his soul in this evil world, before the judgment day comes.

The Bible says, the name of the Lord Jesus Christ, is given for our salvation (Acts 4:12), and this is done through baptism in Jesus' name. A sinner washes away their sins in the blood of Jesus Christ, and puts on Christ, the only garment of righteousness that gives man a ticket to the *feast of the Lamb of God*. (see Matthew 22:1-14) If you are not baptised in Jesus' name for the remission of your sins then you are without a wedding garment as stated in the Scripture above.

Every human being has the right to the son-ship through Jesus Christ, the son of God. The Bible says God has given us life, we who were dead in sin through Adam, and the life is in His Son, he who has the Son has life and he who has not the Son has no life in him. (Roman 5:12)

This is the revelation of the salvation of man, given to the disciples of Jesus Christ. This is why they did not go about preaching and baptising in the titles of the Father, the Son, and of the Holy Spiritt, because they had received the revelation that Jesus Christ is the second Adam, the Lord God from heaven. God in His mercy did not leave man whom He created in His own image for His worship, to die in sin.

As the omniscient God, He made adequate provision for our salvation before the fall of Adam and Eve whom He knew would fail Him. The greatest gift that God has given to man is Himself; that is; the Creator gave out His life for man, His creature, in giving him eternal life.

Behold what manner of love the Father hath bestowed upon us, that we should be called the sons of God: therefore the world knoweth us not, because it knew him not. Beloved, now are we the sons of God and it do not yet appear what we shall be: but we know that, when he shall appear, we shall be like him; for we shall see him as he is. (1John 3:1-2)

Self Examination

Therefore we ought to give the more earnest heed to the things which we have heard, lest at any time we should let them slip. For if the word spoken by angels was steadfast, and every transgression and disobedience received a just recompense of reward; How shall we escape, if we neglect so great salvation; which at the first began to be spoken by the Lord, and was confirmed unto us by them that heard him; God also bearing them witness, both with signs and wonders, and with divers miracles, and gifts of the Holy Ghost, according to his own will? (Hebrews 2:1-4)

Examine yourselves, whether ye be in the faith; prove your own selves, how that Jesus Christ is in you, except ye be reprobates? (2 Corinthians 13:5)

The purpose of the suffering of our Lord Jesus Christ on the Calvary cross is to bring salvation to man and nothing more. The cross speaks of salvation or damnation, and it depends on which one you choose. The cross gives us understanding. The front of the cross, where Jesus Christ was crucified, is where the throne of God's grace is, and is from where He saves the world, but at the back of the cross is the judgment seat of the Lord, which is without mercy.

You can understand this better if you recall the position of the Mercy Seat of God in the tabernacle in the Old Testament. It is a good thing for every living human being to know that Jesus Christ is the saviour of the living and the judge of the dead. It does not matter how great your sin is, if you turn to Him for salvation, He will save you. But, if you reject the Gospel of Jesus Christ and die in your sin, there is no more mercy for you, and you face eternal destruction in the *Lake of Fire*.

Apostle Paul, the teacher chosen by our Lord, Jesus Christ, made the whole matter clear to us by saying *if any man be in Christ he is a new creature*. (2 Corinthians 5:17), confirming what Jesus Christ had said, *I am the Way the Truth and the Life, and no one goes to the Father but by me.* (John 14:6) We enter into Christ through baptism in the name of Jesus Christ from where we become Abraham's seed.

For ye are all the children of God by faith in Christ Jesus. For as many of you as have been baptised into Christ have put on Christ. There is neither Jew nor Greek, there is neither bond nor free, there is neither male nor. Female; for ye are all one in Christ Jesus. And if ye be Christ's, then are ye Abraham's seed and heirs according to the promise. (Galatians 3:26-29)

Understanding the above Scriptures is a blessing unto you. The true identity of a Christian is the uniform of righteousness, which he puts on through baptism in the name of our Lord Jesus. The Bible says there is no other name given among men in heaven, on earth and under the earth whereby we shall be saved. (Acts 4:12) We must understand that the name of Jesus Christ is not only for miracles, signs and wonders, but also for salvation. It is written that: *the name of the Lord is a strong tower, the righteous runs into it and is saved.* (Proverbs 18:10)

True servants of the Lord will tell you that the greatest miracle or healing that a man can receive, is the salvation of his soul, through water baptism in Jesus' name for the remission of his sins, and the regeneration of his dead spirit through the Holy Spirit baptism in the name of Jesus Christ.

Then opened he their understanding, that they might understand the scripture. And said unto them, thus it is written, and thus it behoved Christ to suffer, and to rise from the dead the third day. And that repentance and remission of sins should be preached in his name among all nations, beginning at Jerusalem. And ye are witnesses of these things. (Luke 24:45-48)

The disciples of Jesus Christ were chosen and had their eyes opened unto the mysteries of salvation. They preached repentance from sins and baptism in Jesus' name for the remission of sin, to the world. Through their teachings and preaching, they were first called *Christians* (followers of Jesus Christ,) in Antioch because of their doctrine and their lifestyle. That has become the name of believers and the followers of Jesus Christ, or the Church, which forms the reference point for Christians today to detect any falsehood in Christendom. Many miracle seekers, in search of power, have ended in *Egypt*, the kingdom of darkness, and are receiving power from *Pharaoh* - the devil - who covers them with his spirit through deceiving miracles.

Woe to the rebellious children, saith the Lord, that take counsel, but not of me; and that cover with a covering, but not of my spirit, that they may add sin to sin: That walk to go down into Egypt, and have not asked at my mouth; to strengthen themselves in the strength of Pharaoh, and to trust in the shadow of Egypt! Therefore shall the strength of Pharaoh be your shame, and the trust in the shadow of Egypt your confusion. (Isaiah 30:1-3)

And I saw three unclean spirits like frogs come out of the mouth of the dragon, and out of the mouth of the beast, and out of the mouth of the false prophet. For they are the spirits of devils, working miracles, which go forth unto the kings of the earth and of the whole world, to gather them to the battle of that great day of God Almighty. Behold, I come as a thief. Blessed is he that watcheth, and keepeth his garments, lest he walk naked, and they see his shame. (Revelation 16:13-14)

Jesus Christ is not coming for any denomination, but for His children who are born again, in His name, have His spirit and live a holy life. This is what He commanded His disciples to preach and teach. Satan knows that this truth about the Christian's baptism, is being revealed in these last days and is permeating the Church. He is using unstable people who are afraid to lose their members if they tell them the truth about baptism in Jesus' name and not in the names of the Father, Son and Holy Spirit. They teach that the two baptisms are the same. You can be baptised in the name of the Father, the Son and the Holy Ghost, or in the name of Jesus; there is nothing wrong about this.

It is because of these people that we have the following Scriptures:

And it came to pass, that, while Apollos was at Corinth, Paul having passed through the upper coasts came to Ephesus: and finding certain disciples, He said unto them, Have ye received the Holy Ghost since ye believed? And they said unto him, we have not so much as heard whether there be any Holy Ghost. And he said unto them, unto what then were ye baptised? And they said, Unto John's baptism.
Then said Paul, John verily baptised with the baptism of repentance, saying unto the people, that they should believe on him which should come after him, that is, on Christ Jesus. When they heard this, they were baptised in the name of the Lord Jesus. And when Paul had laid his hands upon them, the Holy Ghost came on them; and they spake with tongues, and prophesied. And all the men were about twelve. (Acts 19:1-7)

... for this cause I bow my knees unto the Father of our Lord Jesus Christ, Of whom the whole family in heaven and earth is named. (Ephesians 3:14-15)

There is one body, and one Spirit, even as ye are called in one hope of your calling; One Lord, one faith, one baptism, One God and Father of all, who is above all, and through all and in you all. (Ephesians 4:4-6)

The Bible says God has given us Life, and the life is in His son. (Ephesians 2:5) This is the revelation the Apostles received after the Lord opened their understanding to the scriptures and none of them baptised anyone in the name of the Father, the Son, and Holy Ghost but went straight ahead and baptised converts in Jesus' name for the remission of their sins.

Galatians tells us of our position in our Lord Jesus Christ so I want you to examine yourself whether you are still on the right track to heaven or you have been diverted to the road to hell? Every one sent by God had a message for the people, right from the time of Noah. There is no other message greater than the message of salvation, to bring fallen man back to the Lord.

When the Lord put on *flesh* and came to dwell among men for the purpose of saving man (John 1:4), He left us with a message so every true disciple of Jesus Christ would proclaim the same message the Lord proclaimed, that is, a man must be born again of water and of the Spirit, into His kingdom. For salvation, man is not going to be recreated into the kingdom of God but, must be born again by the second Adam, Jesus Christ.

Adam was the foundation and the father of man the *image of God*, so is Jesus Christ, the second Adam from heaven, the father of all those who are born again in His name. Every family has a name, by which they are identified. The Apostles, led by Apostle Peter, could tell the Pharisees that there is no name under heaven whereby man could be saved other than the name of Jesus Christ, which is very important when it comes to salvation plan of God through His name.

Be it known unto you all, and to all the people of Israel, that by the name of Jesus Christ of Nazareth, whom ye crucified, whom God raised from the dead, even by him doth this man stand here before you whole. This is the stone which was set at nought of you builders, which is become the head of the corner.
Neither is there salvation in any other: for there is none other name under heaven given among men, whereby we must be saved. Now when they saw the boldness of Peter and John, and perceived that they were unlearned and ignorant men, they marveled; and they took knowledge of them, that they had been with Jesus. (Acts 4:10-13)

I marvel that ye are so soon removed from him that called you into the grace of Christ unto another gospel. Which is not another; but there be some that trouble you, and would prevent the gospel of Christ. But though we, or an angel from heaven, preach any other gospel unto you than that which we have preached unto you, let him be accursed.
As we said before, so say I now again, if any man preach any other gospel unto you than that ye have received, let him be accursed. For do I now persuade men, or God? or do I seek to please men? For if I yet pleased men, I

should not be the servant of Christ. (Galatians 1:6-10)

Let us hear the conclusion of the whole matter: *Fear God, and keep his commandments: for this is the whole duty of man. For God shall bring every work into judgment, with every secret thing, whether it be good, or whether it be evil.* (Ecclesiastes 12:13-14)

CHAPTER ELEVEN

Who are my Brethren?

While he yet talked to the people, behold, his mother and his brethren stood without, desiring to speak with him. Then one said unto him, Behold, thy mother and thy brethren stand without, desiring to speak with thee. But he answered and said unto him that told him, who is my mother? And who are my brethren? And he stretched forth his hand toward his disciples, and said; behold my mother and my brethren! For whosoever shall do the will of my Father which is in heaven, the same is my brother, and sister, and mother. (Matthew 12:46-50)

According to the above Scripture, during His ministration, a man approached Jesus and told Him that "your mother and your brethren" are standing outside seeking to talk to you. But Jesus asked the man, "who is my mother, and my brethren?" He turned to His disciples and stretched forth His hand toward them, and said, "Behold my mother, and my brethren." He continued to say, "Whosoever shall do the will of my Father which is in heaven, the same is my brother, sister and mother."

Mary was *highly favoured among women* (Luke 1:28) to be the earthly mother of Jesus Christ and His brethren. We can see plainly from the question, who are my mother and brethren, that those that refuse to be born again as part of the heavenly family, in accordance with and in obedience to the teachings of the New Birth and the will of God, will be rejected and end up in the *lake of fire*. For this simple reason, Jesus said that *in that day many shall say unto me, in your name we cast out demons and did many wonderful things, but I will tell them to depart from me because I do not know you.* (Matthew 7:22)

Jesus makes it plain and clear to His followers that those who are born of flesh are flesh and those who are born of the spirit are spirit. He explained the difference between the sons and daughters of the first Adam, who are flesh and blood *(carnal man or the image of God),* and those of the second Adam - the Lord God from heaven - who are born again with water and of the spirit of Jesus Christ. These have been transformed from the image of God to be the spiritual sons and daughters of God through the New Birth experience while on earth.

How to be born again and live a holy life is the greatest statement from the teachings of our Lord and Saviour, Jesus Christ, so His people will not miss heaven. If we accept the true teaching of the New Birth and humbly search for understanding, we may not be cast out at the end of our struggling to enter His kingdom as one of His children.

If Jesus Christ could deny His mother, brothers, and sisters, this is a direct message to the world and His followers of today who call themselves *Christians*, because of the church they attend. His mother, brothers and sisters had followed Him during His earthly ministry, yet they would be rejected had they refused to be born again with water and of the Spirit in His name and be called His disciples. The Lord Jesus Christ, who came as a Jew (God's people) from the lineage of King David, told Nicodemus, a teacher of the Jews, that he must be born again, before he can enter into the kingdom of Heaven. For what is born of the flesh is flesh and what is born of the Spirit is spirit.

Jesus was simply telling His followers that we were all born into this world through physical fathers and mothers and we have brothers and sisters (worldly family) who are corrupted by the devil through Adam and Eve's disobedience. What will separate us finally is the final destination with Jesus into Heaven if we receive the New Birth through Him. But, if we refuse the new birth, we will remain as the image of God corrupted by the devil through Adam and Eve from the very beginning of time.

Satan's motive for corrupting humanity is to lead them into destruction in the Lake of Fire. If anybody rejects the New Birth of water and of the Spirit that God provides through His Son Jesus Christ; that soul will be condemned forever to the Lake of Fire. (Revelation 19:20) It does not matter what name we call ourselves or the title we give ourselves in ministry. If we refuse to be born again of water and of the Spirit in Jesus' name, God will see us as the children of the devil.

This is why Jesus says: *Ye are of your father the devil, and the lusts of your father ye will do. He was a murderer from the beginning, and abode not in the truth, because there is no truth in him. When he speaketh a lie, he speaketh of his own: for he is a liar, and the father of it. And because I tell you the truth, ye believe me not.* John 8:44-45

The Lake of Fire is not the will of God for man, and for this reason, He has established His heavenly kingdom in this world; to save the world (men) unto Himself. Jesus told the people that whosoever shall do the will of His Father who is in heaven, because left to God alone every man shall be saved into heaven His dwelling place where there is joy everlasting prepare for His children. (Matthew 7:21-23)

Jesus said it takes the New Birth for one to be part of the heavenly brethren *(family)*. If He made that statement about His own mother and brethren, and pointed a finger at His disciples, saying this is my mother and my brethren, it was to give us the understanding that the *New Birth* must be the foundation of the message from God to a fallen world *(sinners)*. This message of being born again must be given by true servants of God before any other things, like prophecies, miracles, healings, blessings and so forth. The greatest miracle is for a man to accept the gospel and save his soul from the everlasting punishment in the Lake of Fire.

Although all such things are good, the main purpose of Jesus' coming into this evil and sinful world is for the salvation of souls of men from the eternal sufferings in the Lake of Fire.

The question is, can Jesus call us brethren because we say we are Christians - His followers? If He could deny His own mother, brothers and sisters in the *flesh,* for the New Birth, what will He say nto us who are far away from the heavenly brotherhood, if we refuse to be born again of water and of the Spirit in His name yet still call ourselves brethren in the kingdom of God?

The Bible says Jesus Christ is the same *yesterday; today and forever.* (Hebrews 13:8) The *born again* process set apart the disciples of Jesus Christ who were Jews, from their Jewish nationals, and made them heavenly citizens as Christians known as saints. Is it not still separating physical families today?

Many people are rejected by their families for accepting Jesus Christ as their personal Lord and Saviour. It is the promise of the New Birth that will make the true Christians, brethren and heavenly citizens. The question that Jesus asked, *who are my brethren and my mother*, should give the servants of God the understanding that God is not overly interested in whatever we do in His church other than to be *born again* as His children for the future salvation of our souls.

You must be born again into the Christian family with Jesus Christ, Himself, being the father, rather than just being a member of a church, and not part of the body of Christ. Israel is the nation that originated from Jacob, known as Israel, and a direct grandson of Abraham, so Jews know themselves as the children of one man. Christianity also makes the people of God one family, and the children of one father, Jesus Christ, throughout the world. This is the reason so many countries around the world worship Jesus Christ in these end times.

Jesus Christ (A Jew) Died for the Whole World.

The Jews are the most rejected people on earth. The wicked are accepted before the Jews - God's chosen nation here on earth. Who is behind this?

Is it because they reject their Messiah or has their God rejected them forever? Some Christian organisations claim to love Jesus Christ, but hate His brethren, the Jews, because they rejected their Messiah and handed Him over to the Gentiles to be crucified while they stood and watched. The Good News to the Gentile world was Jesus' rejection by His brethren the Jews. Understanding is the foundation of relationship. After His resurrection, the Lord open the understanding of His disciples to understand the Scriptures. (Luke 24:45)

If Christians worldwide understand that the Jews have been rejected temporarily under the church dispensation (the *dispensation of grace*) because God is bringing in the Gentiles (the other nations) to Himself, that alone would bring comfort to the Jews. They would be loved and cherished everywhere by their brethren, the Christians, who are known as the *spiritual* Jews throughout the world.

The truth of the matter is that Jesus Christ, the Lord God from Heaven, whom Apostle Paul called the *second Adam,* was born in Israel to draw the *other nations* unto Himself through His death on the cross, so that they can have access to the New Jerusalem as spiritual Jews.

For I would not, brethren, that ye should be ignorant of this mystery, lest ye should be wise in your own conceits; that blindness in part is happened to Israel, until the fullness of the Gentiles be come in. And so all Israel shall be saved; as it is written. There shall come out of Zion the Deliverer, and shall turn away ungodliness from Jacob: For this is my covenant unto them, when I shall take away their sins. As concerning the gospel, they are enemies for your sakes: but as touching the election, they are beloved for the fathers' sakes. For the gifts and calling of God are without repentance. (Romans 11:25-29)

Apostle Paul, the former leader of the persecutors of the Apostolic faith, interceded on behalf of his brethren, the Jews, after he was delivered from the Jewish religion, that they also might be saved. He received revelation that God has blinded them in order to reach out to the Gentiles (other nations apart from Israel) in fulfillment of His covenant with Abraham; making him the father of many nations. We see that the Jewish rejection of their Messiah (God who came in the flesh), brought a curse upon them while bringing blessings to the Gentiles who received Him through the gospel and became part of God's people.

If there are people who must support the Jews going back to Israel for the fulfillment of the end time prophecy, they must be the Christians, known as the *spiritual* Jews. Apostle Paul, in the days of his missionary works, sent contributions made by the church to be given to the brethren in the church in Jerusalem. (Romans 15:26)

Today we have Apostles, Prophets and many men of God who boast of their physical blessings from the pulpit of God without remembering their suffering brethren in the land of Israel, with their substance and prayers. The Bible talks about the New Jerusalem and this is not for the physical Jews, but for the spiritual Jews, both Israelites and Gentiles, *the other nations,* who are born again into Christ. This is where both the Jews and the Gentiles come together as one spiritual nation of God's people.

The Church must go back to the preaching and teaching of the New Birth and holiness, so that lost souls can be saved into the kingdom of God. If you are not born again according to the preaching and teachings of Jesus Christ and His disciples, now is the appointed time. Now is the day of salvation. Check your salvation against the Scriptures and save yourself from this *untoward generation*, as Apostle Peter said in Acts 2:38-42 and 1 Peter 3:18-21.

EPILOGUE

The preaching and the teaching of prosperity, miracles and healings without the New Birth are leading many people, looking for their salvation, unknowingly into destruction. Jesus Christ, the Saviour, said, *seek ye first the kingdom of God and all its righteousness and all the other things shall be added unto you*. (Matthew 6:33)

With this understanding, anyone looking for salvation must know that the other things, without the New Birth, are useless. The church of Jesus Christ must be taught to understand that Jesus Christ is coming to take His children home to Himself, and not churches or religious people.

<u>Nicodemus, you must be born again</u> answers the question: who are my brethren, my mother and my sisters? With this understanding, we need to find the answer to the question of our salvation.

God bless you, Reader, for your new understanding in search of the genuineness of your salvation. The understanding that God provides through His son, Jesus Christ. What will stop the Church from condemning one another in unity, is for us to understand ourselves as the children of God through Jesus Christ, the son of God, and as one nation of God just like the nation of Israel.

We have one faith, one Lord who is the God of all creation; His name is Jesus Christ of Nazareth. Let us exalt Him together in holiness and oneness of mind.

www.ingramcontent.com/pod-product-compliance
Lightning Source LLC
Chambersburg PA
CBHW061039050726
47592CB00004B/1506